M000118657

To:

HASAN & Family

Mutlulukla Okuyun!

Berd Bozgu

Theresa M. Bozgu &

Reprogram Your Brain for Happiness & Progressive Mental Health

Social Brain Healing, DNA Extraction & Strategies for Ending Rage

Theresa Boza

authorHOUSE®

AuthorHouse™
1663 Liberty Drive
Bloomington, IN 47403
www.authorhouse.com
Phone: 1 (800) 839-8640

Copyrighted © by Theresa Boza. All rights reserved.

No part of this book may be reproduced, stored in a retrieval system, or
transmitted by any means without the written permission of the author.

Published by AuthorHouse   12/08/2015

ISBN: 978-1-5049-5098-5 (sc)
ISBN: 978-1-5049-5099-2 (hc)
ISBN: 978-1-5049-5097-8 (e)

Library of Congress Control Number: 2015915474

Print information available on the last page.

Any people depicted in stock imagery provided by Thinkstock are models,
and such images are being used for illustrative purposes only.
Certain stock imagery © Thinkstock.

This book is printed on acid-free paper.

Because of the dynamic nature of the Internet, any web addresses or links contained in
this book may have changed since publication and may no longer be valid. The views
expressed in this work are solely those of the author and do not necessarily reflect the
views of the publisher, and the publisher hereby disclaims any responsibility for them.

The anecdotes in this book are from clients seen by Theresa Boza LCSW-R for behavioral health
services. In all cases the names and identifying information have been changed to protect their
right to privacy. The purpose of the publication is to provide education, encourage and inspire
for self-transformation or self-healing. Neither the author nor publisher shall have any liability
or responsibility to any person or entity with respect to any loss, consequence, or damage caused
or alleged to be caused, directly or indirectly, by the information contained in this book.

CONTENTS

Chapter 9: DNA EXTRACTION & HAPPY NEURAL

DEDICATION

I am dedicating this book to great leaders who epitomized a life's search for a peaceful, diverse society and world: Mahatma Gandhi of India, Dr. Martin Luther King Jr. of the United States; Dr. Anta Cheikh Diop, who taught me that African people had been the first humans and had developed a civilization rooted in science, medicine, written language, architecture, and a culture of kinship and loving kindness towards others. There are others that you will read about such as President Nelson Mandela of South Africa. I also dedicate this book to the many adolescent clients I have treated over the years who changed their aggressive styles to a lifestyle that is more peaceful and mindfulness oriented, despite highly traumatic histories.

It is also dedicated to my son, Khalif, who has always maintained a peaceful stance despite various physical and learning challenges he had to overcome. He taught me the power of the brain to transcend birth injuries and discrimination. My adolescent clients taught me the power of the neurotropic dynamic of psychotherapy that is geared to overcoming loss and abuse with a focus on strengthening the wise mind with mindfulness awareness, cognitive growth, and peaceful solutions. And to my husband Birol of twenty-five years, at the time of this writing, who has always loved and encouraged me. I also want to thank my cousin Jesse Mayfield, who wrote the book Away From My Mother's Watchful Eyes and gave me tips on how to get published; and Stuart Moss of the Nathan S. Kline Institute for Psychiatric Research.

PREFACE

Accepting trials and tribulations is a part of life's journey especially in a world full of pain and hate. You must be the peaceful warrior and change for the sake of your progressive mental and physical health, happiness, with non-violence (in all its forms—verbal, physical, emotional), so that you can say, "I have contributed to the Spirit of the Planet Earth with loving kindheartedness and non-violence." One act of violence or rage sets off a volcano of suffering spreading emotional pathology. In a world full of suffering, hate, disappointments, and retaliation, to achieve this contribution requires reprogramming the brain to achieve progressive happiness and progressive mental health, which leads to a positive spiritual contribution to the world of peace and human kinship.

In this book I refer to the Human Family. All humans, whatever their features, are currently classified by anthropologists and biologists as belonging to one species, Homo sapiens or hybrid Homo sapiens. All humankind can interbreed because we all share an ancestor; thus, we have a capacity to love each other because we have so much in common, biologically. All humans share nearly 100 percent of the same genetic materials.

The Human Family based on ancestral karma is defined for this book as:

Nubian: The First Humans

Caucasian: The Imperialistic Humans

Mongolian: The Spiritual Humans

The Hybrid Human: Any combination of the three, physically or culturally. To learn more about the First humans and Hybrid Humans: http://www.pbs.org/first-peoples/episodes/africa/ Or see Dr. Spencer Wells—Journey of Man: A Genetic Odyssey.

All humans come from cultural communities that define their language, geography, and lifestyle. Terms like Black and White have contributed to labeling people; they have contributed to violence, depression, and poor mental health in our American multicultural community. This type of labeling to separate and divide people, versus terms of relatedness, contributes to hate, retaliatory stress, and trauma. It also impacts the wiring of your social brain. Your social brain starts forming neural circuits at birth, which impacts your mental health, and your happiness. Stereotypes and labeling can impact the brain programming for depression and poor self-worth as you will learn from this book. You will also learn that you can reprogram your brain for happiness and for progressive mental health.

INTRODUCTION

Do you have issues of poor anger management, depression, anxiety, failure in your work or your love life, social phobias, financial problems, feelings of hopelessness, or just a lack of happiness in your life? If so, it is highly likely that your emotional mind, the limbic system and amygdala functions of your brain, have been impacted. If you have these issues, you may have or may be experiencing some traumatic or hurtful events, consciously or unconsciously.

Traumatic events can occur during childhood, adolescence, or adulthood; and you may have no conscious awareness of how to heal from your trauma or how your social brain was or is impacted. Unless you reprogram your trauma or hurt feelings for self-healing, you can become trapped in your anger and need for revenge, which is retaliatory stress. In essence, you become addicted to being angry: you get loud, curse, throw things, blame others, and you may have a malevolent look. In the extreme, your facial expression becomes like the expression of the mother in the movie, *Precious.* Or, you may become addicted to being anxious or depressed and may resort to compulsive overeating, drugs, alcohol, social-isolation, excessive clutter in your home, self-criticism, or self-injury. Your anger and addiction to negative emotions result in the amygdala system of your brain becoming, in layman's terms: impaired and depleted of the happiness and peaceful neurochemicals in your brain.

Anger is an infantile and biological emotion. Anger is Infantile because it is one of our first emotions. If the infant does not have needs met related to attachment, nurturance, and happy-face contacts, he or she will yell and scream in the infantile way. If this continues, the infant's brain will be impacted and the neurochemicals and wiring processes of the brain that allow for a happy and peaceful life will be impacted (Schore, 2001). Many of us spend most of our lives reacting to anger in some infantile manner.

If you get mad and throw something, punch a wall, hit someone, or worse yet, kill or nearly kill someone, your brain has been affected and depleted of the neurochemicals that would allow you to respond differently to painful experiences. The neurochemicals or hormones for happiness and calmness are natural opioids, oxytocin, endorphin, dopamine, and serotonin. Stress and angry thoughts blocks the release of the happiness and calmness hormones. With these hormones in your mind, you can reprogram yourself for happiness and peace or you can continue creating a state of mind for poor mental health, unhappiness, and chronic agitation, which only depletes these neurochemicals.

In the world we live in, bad things happen to most people. I know they happen to me. I want to let you know that you can withstand the pain of bad things. If you don't withstand the pain of bad things and take control of your emotions, most likely you will have one disappointment and hurtful experience after the other, one failure after the other. Subsequently, your social brain becomes full of negative thoughts, and these impair your emotional functioning, your happiness, and your mental health. You will resort to taking medication, using drugs or alcohol, or compulsively eating to medicate your social emotional brain. Food, alcohol, sex, drugs, and even the nicotine in cigarettes temporarily provide neurochemicals like endorphin, serotonin, natural opioids, oxytocin, and dopamine that help you feel calm, happy, confident, and hopeful. However there are healthier ways to feel good and keep these neurochemicals alive in your body and mind, which you will learn based on scientific studies.

Have you ever had an extremely emotional day, after which you ate tons of your favorite food or drank too much alcohol? Thoughts of searching and planning for that delicious strawberry shortcake created dopamine (a happy neurochemical) in the brain. We all have moments when we are upset. But I am also referring to chronic, unresolved anger and depression because of bad situations that you have no control over, such as a drug-addicted mother, an absent father, a sibling in prison, discrimination on the job, domestic violence, a child who is out of control, parents who want perfection, unethical teachers or professors, and so on. That's why I emphasize *progressive* mental health and *progressive* happiness.

In a world full of hate, discrimination, and displaced retaliation, if you are too happy or too trusting, you will be scammed and hurt. Truly good people project that others are like them. However, after being scammed and hurt, truly good people may become distrustful and isolated; they may seek retaliation and/or pollute their brains with negative thoughts, which subsequently impact the mind and body.

This scenario is not necessary; if you learn a few skills to minimize negative thoughts and maximize positive thoughts. Or if you learn to keep alive thoughts that heal; you can keep your mental health stable. Just as individuals work on their physical health, this book is your personal trainer for your mental health. You need to stabilize yourself, because bad things happen to most people, and most of us experience negative reactions even if we are truly good people.

Negative reactions increase stress hormones in the body that lead to states of fight or flight, and this impacts the neurochemistry of the social brain. The brain has a negativity bias; so bad experiences stay planted in our brains and negatively impact mental health and happiness (Hanson, 2011). We are far more likely to remember that someone called us a bad name at work than that someone said thank you. This negativity bias creates negative thoughts that can accumulate over time and stay in the social brain, leading to depression, rage, and even violent behaviors. Subsequently, chronic negative energy can be transmitted culturally from one generation to the next. So, the angry mom has an angry son who is prone to negative reactions.

I am a psychotherapist who uses a concept called social brain healing, cognitive-spiritual therapy, and guided imagery techniques for ancestral regression to teach my clients how to live happily in a world that is beautiful, advanced, and offers great opportunity, but is also a world full of pain. I let my clients know that bad things have happened in our world, but there are ways of thinking and transforming emotional pain. I have worked with numerous clients and mental health patients of all ethnic groups, but especially with African Americans and Hispanic Americans. I've worked with children, adolescents, adults, couples, and families who resort to aggression (verbal or physical) and even violence when they experience emotional pain. Emotional pain and reactions of rage— yelling, screaming, cursing, and fighting—affect your mental health, just like a diet of excessive sugar and carbohydrates affect your physical health.

Most people are more tuned into their physical health than their mental health. Have you ever been in a relationship that triggered profound anger so that you hit someone or called them hurtful names or cheated out of revenge? Repeated acts of these types of behaviors—yelling, hitting, lying, cursing—become personality traits. Your negative mental state becomes your personality traits through a brain process reported by neurologists: *Brain neurons that fire together wire together* (Arden 2010 p.8).

If you are struggling with poor anger management, depression, anxiety, lack of success at work or in your love life, social phobias, financial problems, feelings of hopelessness, or just a lack of happiness, know that these are signs that your mental health could benefit from some of the knowledge and interventions you will learn in this book. Sometimes people hurt us and probably deserve punishment, but being the deliverer of the punishment may result in serious consequences for your social brain and, subsequently, for your emotional mental health.

Trying to cope with the pain of the external human world we all live in is not easy; I'm with you all the way on this, but feeling sorry and hopeless or raging and retaliating can result in poor mental health. I say this realizing that you may be facing a stressful divorce, have just been fired unfairly from your job or been evicted from your apartment. You may have learned that you are HIV-positive or obtained an STD while in a monogamous relationship (so you thought) or just learned that you have cancer. You may have been given an unfair failing grade at school despite studying hard and aiming for an A. Maybe you just learned that your wife is cheating on you with your best friend; maybe you have been imprisoned unfairly or have just lost someone you love deeply (a parent, child or spouse). The list of possible painful experiences goes on and on.

Bell Hooks, a native South African who grew up in the apartheid environment of South Africa, gives a descriptive illustration of the impact of painful experiences and negative emotions in her book *Killing Rage, An End to Racism.* While traveling with a friend, she suffered from racial harassment by airline stewardesses. Ms. Bell and her friend had purchased first-class tickets and, after being seated together, her friend was forced to give up the seat for a Caucasian male, who then sat next to Ms. Hooks. The experience triggered a negative emotion: killer rage. In her book, she states, *"I felt a killing rage. I wanted to stab him softly, to shoot him with the gun I wished I had in my purse. And as I watched his pain, I would say to him tenderly, 'Racism hurts'"* (Hooks, 1995, p. 9). Racism or xenophobia is an illness, and a component of overt narcissism, in which an individual hurts others unconsciously or consciously.

Yes, painful experiences can hurt and can lead to suffering and even to killer rage. I hear about it every day from my clients and from the TV or the local radio station. Do you have rage? If so, you are suffering, and your brain is being affected. However, you don't have to resort to suffering. In this book you will learn the human skills of individuals like **Nelson Mandela**, also a native South African, who withstood painful experiences and effectively coped with twenty-seven years of unfair imprisonment due to the political actions of overt narcissism and xenophobia. The skills you will learn allowed him to survive. And when he was released from prison, his social brain had developed and maintained healthy neural connections and neurochemicals, which resulted in progressive happiness and progressive mental health. He reframed his thinking and minimized the unhealthy neurochemicals of negative thoughts, which impact your physical health and mental health.

To heal your mental health you need to know the truth of the human race, our relatedness and your ancestral history. DNA as data storage allows you to incorporate the spiritual wisdom of your ancestors and delete the traits that interfere with emotional health for yourself and for others. Imagine the wealth of what you can learn if you access the spiritual energy of ancestors who successfully overcame harsh traumas. Learning from individuals like Nelson Mandela is a strategy called ancestral regression, which you will learn about in this book. No matter what your painful experience, what you learn here will help you effectively create neurochemicals, such as endorphins, serotonin, and dopamine, by changing your thought patterns and learning skills that lead to social brain healing.

Historically, we had many great leaders, like Nelson Mandela, who experienced bad things and the pains of oppression, racism, poverty, discrimination, and apartheid and yet achieved substantial successes. They opened schools and were leaders of universities, presidents of their countries, inventors, business owners, and humanitarians. You will learn about their pain and their human strategies for progressive mental health and happiness. These coping strategies and positive thought patterns and intentions have not been culturally transmitted or written about in a way that provides self-healing skills.

In this book, I seek to bring these human therapeutic coping strategies to life for my readers. I seek to forward the notion of social brain healing with loving kindness; DNA extraction of hate, violence, revenge, rage; and ending labels like Black and White, which deplete your happiness. I seek creating words like human family; our genealogical relatedness, kinship with all humanoids and reprogram the brain for love and acceptance of self, variety and diversity.

No matter what your painful experiences have been, you can start today to create happy hormones in your brain and body by changing the way you think about the world. Many of my clients have experienced some form of trauma in childhood or adulthood;

and some have strong proclivities towards anger and violence, either verbal or physical. I worked for over ten years on a secure care unit with aggressive male adolescents. Prior to my arrival on the unit, the patients had barricaded the clinical staff and attempted to take over the unit. Within one year of my arrival as a clinician on the unit, significant changes were made, and this unit drastically reduced the number of aggressive incidents. The clients had learned about the positive energy channel in their brains for kinship with all life forms and made good use of it.

As a human family we have done wonders in our growth towards physical health, ending various physical illnesses and diseases. Today, people are living much longer lives. We have done wonders in our economic progress by improving the physical quality of life with new technologies that are being invented every day. We can see the many wonders—jet planes, tall buildings/malls, cars with TV, smart phones, and beautiful villas on the beach—all created by members of the human family. However, as a human family, we have not made the same progress in our mental health. Even today, we have police officers killing innocent citizens; parents killing their children; children killing their parents; spouses killing each other; individuals killing for a pair of sneakers; individuals killing because they don't like the color of a person's complexion or sexual orientation or the way he/she chooses to believe or not believe in God. Or Individuals killing for financial enrichment; and bombing and killing others for their own self-interest. We are far from a civilization that knows and respects the biological fact that we are all related, cousins, if you will, and thus as humanoid family we do have the capacity to "love thyself" and are equally able to "love thy neighbors," neighbors who are both near and distant from thyself.

We can fly planes; we have found cures for polio and for diphtheria, which is now almost non-existent. We can build tall buildings, walk on the moon, but we are weak in our ability to control anger, an infantile emotion, and weak in our ability for loving kindness and feeling empathy for others. This human weakness, this inability to feel loving kindness and empathy for others is due to a social mental illness—narcissism—both overt and covert narcissism.

The stories you will read about in this book is solely for the purpose of: self-awareness, historical facts, truths, forgiveness and healing the social brain for loving kindness; and having an understanding related to the extraction of the angry brain which depletes the happy neurochemicals. The visualization imagery method that you will learn about referred to as Ancestral Regression is geared towards bringing together the human family for healing of ancestral karmas for peace and to foster a positive attitude for financial independence and a successful life free from rage, retaliation, and victim mentality. Ancestral karma can be based on the success of our spiritual ancestors who successfully withstood pain and traumas with dignity.

CHAPTER 1

NARCISSISM, SELF-INTEREST & VIOLENCE — WHAT YOU NEED TO KNOW

The pain in the world we may have no control over, but this book

will guide you to gain control over yourself and your responses to

painful experiences. Why is this so important? Painful experiences

are unavoidable in the world we live in, which is polluted with

the silent social mental illness called *narcissism*. Because of

this silent social mental illness, many people react intensely to

painful experiences by retaliating aggressively, which they view

as normal or justifiable; alternatively, many react through flight

into depression and isolation. Such reactions destroy mental

health, as well as the mental health of others.

Robert Kiyosaki, author of *Rich Dad Poor Dad,* warns that the
biggest criminals or con artists you will ever meet often appear to be
honest, are well-educated, are often attractive, may have advanced
degrees, hold high positions of leadership, but may lack moral
character (Kiyosaki &Trump, 2011). Many wealthy people are rarely
convicted of any crimes or held accountable for wrong-doing. In our
society, we often view rich, beautiful people in powerful positions

as God or believe what they believe about themselves—that they are superior people. On the other hand, we tend to equate poor, unattractive, uneducated people with criminals.

Many people in top leadership positions with the power to hire and fire cause painful experiences, lack empathy, lack emotional and spiritual maturity, and lack strength of character when it comes to the needs of others. This kind of leadership may account for why there is so little progress in the area of mental health. Individuals who engage in such self-interest behaviors that hurt others have the personality of narcissism, which I refer to as a social mental illness. These narcissistic individuals who appear to be so honest and who often are well educated can turn into criminals when things do not go their way. Social scientists have found that narcissists steeped in superiority can become criminals when their egos are threatened in some way (Baumeister, Heatherton, & Tice, 1993; Baumeister, Smart, & Boden, 1996; Morf & Rhodewalt 2001).

Social scientists have observed a relationship between narcissism and aggression (Fossati, Borroni, Eisenberg, and Maffei, 2010). Many narcissists have irrational beliefs about their superiority and about their entitlement (Sullivan & Geaslin, 2001). Twenge and Campbell (2003) became interested in the issue of narcissism following the school shootings at Columbine High School. The two boys who were the shooters were known to be school bullies (Shoels, 1999). Based on quotes discovered after the shooting incident, it was clear that the boys perceived that their peers rejected them; and, yes, this was true because of the boys' bullying and racist behaviors. The boys' statements resembled statements that have been used to test for narcissism. The things the boys said indicated narcissistic traits and extreme anger arousal after social rejection.

In his book *The Culture of Narcissism,* (1979), Christopher Lasch wrote about the increase in narcissistic personalities in America. His publication led to interest in new research into narcissism and added narcissism as a personality disorder in the *Diagnostic and Statistical Manual of Mental illnesses.*

The seven features of narcissism are (Emmons, 1984; Emmons, 1987):

- Self-sufficiency
- Superiority
- Vanity
- Grandiosity
- Entitlement
- Exhibitionism
- Exploitation

Most of us know about our human family's history of imperialism and slavery: individuals who feel superior and entitled will sacrifice the lives of others for self-enrichment and will use their rational minds to justify their actions as normal behavior. Narcissism as a social illness, just like other social illnesses—alcoholism, for example—can be transmitted from one person to another, from one family group to another, and from one generation to another.

Without an understanding of the social illness narcissism; and of knowing how it functions in your life and in our human world, you are just not immunized against the long-term emotional destruction that narcissism can cause. You may not have this illness, but you may be living or working with someone who does. Without awareness of this social illness, you are at high risk for an emotional life filled with anxiety, depression, fear, distrust, negative thoughts, negative response patterns, and brain chemistry that create a chronic bleeding of negative neural transmitters, which results in physical and mental illnesses, such as hypertension, diabetes, obesity, depression, panic attacks, anxiety, and rage.

With knowledge and strategies, you can avoid the debilitating impact on your social brain due to the behaviors of others who have this social illness. However, first you must be aware that narcissism exists and has existed for centuries. It is a silent social mental illness, but it produces a loud whack to the emotional minds of others. Many individuals with this social mental illness narcissism are church-going people and are well-educated. They are your co-workers; they are professionals, CEOs, mothers and fathers, and husbands and wives.

Consider this historical event—a true story:

THE CASE OF THE LYNCHING OF ARTHUR STEVEN IN 1933

Arthur was an African American man who reportedly dated and had a sexual relationship with Iona, a European-American farm girl. He was accused of murdering her, but this was never proven in any court of law. Narcissistic parenting exists in many cultures, and if a child of narcissistic parents has a sexual relationship with someone the parents do not agree to, then both the child and the partner may be at risk of death. Immediately after the death of Iona, who had a sexual relationship with Arthur—someone her parents did not agree to—the girl's neighbors, led by Iona's father, organized, overtook the jail, and captured Arthur. He was tortured, killed, and hung from a tree, naked. The mob decided on a style of torture that consisted of ten hours of torture and castration, and Arthur was even forced to eat his genitals. Red-hot irons were plunged into his body, and he was ultimately choked to death by hanging (Monte, 1980).

The people of the town appeared to approve of this behavior and lynching, saw nothing horrible or frightening about this behavior. Subsequently, others in the community on Iona's father's side, but who had absolutely nothing to do with Iona or Arthur, started to physically attack and torture innocent Nubian people from Arthur's section of town. For an entire day, the lynch mob physically wreaked havoc on innocent Native American people of African descent who resided in the town, including women and children. The deputy sheriff and local authorities stated, *"The mob will not be bothered,"* thus providing government and state support for the acts of cruelty, violence and displaying a blatant lack of any remorse or empathy towards innocent humans (Monte, 1980, p. 596).

This is a true story. The people who killed and wreaked havoc on the lives of others in this southern American community were church-going, hard-working people, and some were leaders of the community, such as the deputy sheriff and the local authorities.

That happened in 1933. In quite recent years, I was a student at an online university, working to obtain my Ph.D., which focused on aggression, trauma, and narcissism, when I was faced with narcissism. At the time, I was a director at a mental health center, had been in private practice for over ten years, and had a master's degree from Columbia University, an Ivy League school in New York City. I had over twenty years' experience working with aggression and trauma issues in poor and middle-income communities, had a GPA of 3.5, and a 4.0 in my specialty area of research and evaluation. I had over 300 credit hours; nonetheless, I was subjected to deliberate

5

abusive treatment by some professors, including the dean, who were determined that I would not get a Ph.D.

This maltreatment began after I appeared at a face-to-face residency with a professor who hated me. After six years' work on a project that should have taken one year, my dissertation was still being totally dismantled each and every time it was submitted by a professor whose children (both of them) had a history of being arrested. My dissertation was about aggression, trauma, and narcissism in juvenile delinquents, which I guess she did not agree with. Finally, after obtaining over One Hundred and Eighty thousand dollars in student loans, receiving no support from the administration, and enduring the frustration and pain of harassment at this online university, I left without a degree. As an African American, I wasn't lynched like Arthur, nor did I spend twenty-seven years in prison like Mandela, but my face-to-face and online harassment, which lasted over ten years, was truly a traumatic, painful experience. At one point, I even feared for my life.

Today, various forms of traumatic painful experiences can be a part of your life. The more you know about the dynamics of narcissism, the more you are aware that other people will hurt you and traumatize you; the more you know, the more you can effectively protect your mental health and your degree of happiness. Despite having come from a poor background and being raised in Harlem, New York, when I started my Ph.D., I had a goal to help and heal those with a history of abuse, neglect, and discrimination who had anger and retaliation problems. Still, despite repeated dismantling of my dissertation over six years without any valid explanation and now having to pay back loans and interest every month on more than

One Hundred and Eighty thousand dollars for being abused, hated, and harassed at this online university; I am happy. This is what I call progressive happiness; no matter what your emotional pain, you can smile, be happy and kind to others.

CHAPTER 2

OVERT NARCISSISM: TRAITS
OF SUPERIORITY

Many features of narcissism are normal and do not indicate illness. It is when people cause traumatic pain and suffering to enhance themselves; and due to threatened egotism, greed, jealousy, or self-interest, that the social mental illness of overt narcissism is present, but often not recognized.

Individuals with overt narcissism are driven by power and control. I refer to overt narcissism as a hidden social mental illness of self-interest. Some of the main characteristics are superiority; a strong sense of grandiosity; self-sufficiency (which is normal behavior); feelings of entitlement by society or from narcissistic parenting (parents who in a dysfunctional way believe their children are superior to others and therefore entitled to whatever they want by any means possible); vanity; and exploitation of others for self-enrichment. This is a hidden illness; on the outside, the person appears to be perfectly normal. Narcissism is a personality disorder caused primarily by social learning.

I once met a woman who married a perfectly normal man; he was handsome, educated, and stable. One day she came home early and found him in their bedroom with another man. This emotional pathology is a type of autistic self-interest. This husband was only able to blindly think about his own needs, not his wife's needs and how this would impact her, and not their marital vows of commitment. Her long-term reaction to this discovery was debilitating. She isolated herself, would not get out of bed, rarely ate food, had profoundly negative thoughts, was nearly mute, and had suicidal ideations. This is suffering. Suffering goes beyond the experience of pain, as reflected in the Buddhist saying, *"Life is full of pain but you don't have to suffer."* She suffered for many years because she did not have knowledge of the social mental illness of overt narcissism. Consequently, her long-term reactions to her husband's behavior became her own mental illness of anxiety and depression.

Many individuals with overt narcissism are unaware that they have a social mental illness because they are highly functional and often highly self-sufficient. Many are admired for their accomplishments. Overt narcissists have attitudes and behaviors of superiority, intense envy of others, especially those who are different from them or their narrow associations. Overt narcissistic personality traits may be rooted in narcissistic parenting (Zamostny, Slyter, & Rios, 1993); or they may be rooted in a culture that promotes one group of people over another. Overt narcissists lack empathy for others (McHoskey, 1995), like the husband who has sex with another man in the same bedroom he shares with his wife.

At one time, the Ku Klux Klan (KKK), a historical organization, had four million Americans who supported their actions. The KKK members felt superior to others, which enabled the members to drive up and kill people and their children and/or burn down their home or place of business. The KKK behaviors are another example of lack of empathy for the emotions of others. Nonetheless, millions of people supported the KKK. Although the organization is not as popular in today's culture, the way of thinking still exists and is damaging to mental health-the volcano of suffering. People in the KKK considered themselves good, normal people. They went to church and raised their children to go to college and get good grades.

Conventional wisdom has regarded low self-esteem as an important cause of violence, but the opposite view, high self-esteem, has been tested and also found to be a factor in anger and aggression (Papps & O'Carroll, 1998; Bushman & Baumeister, 1998). The KKK felt superior, and that was enough justification for violence. The deputy sheriff felt superior, and that was enough justification for violence. The husband with the male lover felt he was entitled to have his needs met, and that was enough justification for infidelity.

CHARACTERISTICS OF THE OVERT NARCISSIST

- Harbors envy and hatred of others, especially if the other is different, as in the example of the KKK.
- Focuses on social comparison. Overt narcissists do not want fair competition; they want control.
- Seeks to be admired, thus will possess likable, friendly, attractive, intelligent behaviors. Generally, self-sufficiency is characterized by self-discipline related to personal desires.
- May have the ability to control aggressive or violent behaviors and channel them for social acceptance, such as becoming a police officer or passing a lie detector test after killing someone. Such individuals marry, are socially accepted, but when their egos are threatened or if they perceived that someone is against them or attempting to block their self enhancement, they exhibit violence in defense of their wounded pride in a disciplined or proactive manner.

- Is highly self-centered.
- The dynamics of threatened egotism is unconscious.
- Engages in narcissistic parenting—teaches directly or indirectly lack of empathy towards others who are different.
- Highly discriminatory
- Is unable to develop concern or empathy for specific people. For example, Milosevic, the Serbian leader, had no empathy for the thousands of people upon whom he inflicted grievous pain and suffering in Kosovo.
- Have an inborn nature to hate others who are different, which has been passed down for generations; I refer to this as **xenophobia**. Some individuals are more prone towards xenophobia, just like some individuals are more prone towards depression or schizophrenia. Terms like racism will not define or correct the problem. Dr. Jerome Kagan reports that individuals have inborn temperaments (Kagan, 2010); and some overt narcissists do have temperaments that are xenophobic. Below is a picture that shows individual's temperament against differences or xenophobia.

- Idealizes and respects aggressive power, exploitation, and even violent behaviors, which leads to amassing power and material wealth.
- Is eager to promote wars or violent solutions to conflicts.
- Considers kindness and goodness as weaknesses.
- Is highly resistant to change.

Overt narcissism and the cycle of entitlement, superiority, and exploitation give rise to retaliatory stress disorder (RSD) and vulnerable narcissism, which are dynamics of covert narcissism.

CHAPTER 3

COVERT NARCISSISM

Individuals with covert narcissism are driven by anger, rage, and revenge. Covert narcissism is trauma-linked narcissism. It leads to traits of depression and rage, which may mimic the psychological features of post-traumatic stress disorder (PTSD) (Simon, 2002); however, covert narcissism also has the features of entitlement, grandiosity, and exploitation.

When your emotional needs as a child are chronically not met by a parent, society, or significant others, faulty wiring of the social brain occurs. The same is true when you experience physical abuse, neglect, abandonment, sexual abuse (touching in ways that made you feel uncomfortable), or emotional abuse (a lack of positive loving statements or support from your family). So, as a teen, were you bullied at school, rejected, or forced to do things that you did not want to do? As an adult, have you felt discriminated against, controlled, felt hopeless or helpless or victimized, or experienced character defamation? Such experiences in childhood or adulthood can lead to covert narcissism and retaliatory stress—an entitled and grandiose feeling that you are justified in getting even, getting back, punishing, or hurting others because you have been hurt. In some people, these experiences lead to a pathological, covert narcissistic justification for hurting or even killing others who have hurt you. This is not the same as self-defense. Usually, in covert narcissism, the retaliation is displaced, and the person injured or killed is not the person who caused the original pain.

Researchers in the field of narcissism have described trauma experiences during the early grandiosity phases (from birth to around age seven) as resulting in narcissistic insult or injury, which later in life may be characterized by a pathological split of the personality structure, forming the "two faces of narcissism" (Wink, 1991). The grandiose, exhibitionistic, conscious mind of the covert narcissist may seek admiration, recognition, and attention through inappropriate behavior or outrageous dress, hairstyle, etc. On the other hand, the vulnerable, self-critical, victimized mind of the covert narcissist is characterized by fear and a manic need to defend or fight, or a need for flight via food, drugs, alcohol, sex, or isolation.

The defense mechanism of *splitting* allows you, especially men, to deny the vulnerability of depression; it may be easier to fight back with grandiose entitlement and self-preservation rather than be depressed. Splitting can start with childhood trauma experiences and may damage the behavioral, cognitive, and social abilities of the brain pathways (Perry, 2001). Childhood trauma experiences may result in compulsions for entitled retaliation or repetition of the abusive experiences, later in the life cycle (Miller, 1979; Miller, 2002). Covert narcissism stems from emotional deprivation and abuse (physical, sexual, and verbal); this is trauma-linked narcissism (Simon, 2002; Cohen, 1981). Covert narcissists are self-centered and lack empathy for others (McHoskey, 1995); in some cases, covert narcissists suffer the abuse of family and society and develop an autistic blindness towards the emotions of others (Howell, 2003).

CASE ILLUSTRATION: THE BOY AND THE FANCY SNEAKERS

A fifteen-year-old boy sees some fancy sneakers he wants. Another child is wearing them, so he pulls out a gun and demands them. The smaller child, at gunpoint, takes off his shoes and surrenders them. The fifteen-year-old puts the gun to the child's head, smiles, and pulls the trigger. When he is arrested, the officers are chilled by his apparent lack of remorse. When asked if he would do anything differently if he could turn back the clock, he thinks for a moment and replies, "I would have cleaned my shoes." It was his bloody shoes that led to his arrest. He exhibits regret and disappointment for being caught, but no remorse or empathy for the smaller child he just killed (Perry, 1997, p. 126).

This is an example of trauma-linked narcissism, which leads to emotional vulnerability when infantile narcissistic needs are not met. Freud, the father of psychology, proposed the concept of primary narcissism, which occurs when the infant and child passes through an adaptive phase of egocentric behaviors (Monte, 1980). Yes, we all went through a narcissistic phase when our autonomic nervous system could easily resort to sympathetic activity, such as what you see in the normal behaviors of the Terrible Twos. The **sympathetic** nervous system accelerates behavior and is highly reactive. Opposite to the sympathetic nervous system is the **parasympathetic** nervous system, which seeks to stop inappropriate behaviors and is more calm and responsive. The parasympathetic can turn off the reactive nervous system when we respond with love, support of others, an educated and calm mind.

When the child's emotional and physical needs are not met by a nurturing caregiver during this primary egocentric narcissistic phase (infancy to age three), the infant or child may resort to temper tantrums, yelling, screaming, biting, and kicking. If the child during this phase is exposed to abuse and neglect by a caregiver, these abusive and neglectful interactions can damage the orbitofrontal cortex (OFC) of the brain (Schore, 2001). The **OFC**, in simple terms, regulates emotions and the body. Damage to the OFC in infancy and childhood affects the nervous system, resulting in chronic reactive behaviors or chronic temper tantrums.

The emotional requirements of the narcissistic phase, if not understood by the caregiver, can lead to retaliation against the demanding, self-centered child (for example, severe physical punishment). Even when needs are met, the child may still resort to these behaviors, because having temper tantrums is normal during the narcissistic phase, and no parent can meet every need during this phase. I'm sure you have seen a two-year-old having a temper tantrum when he didn't get his way. Temper tantrums are normal behaviors during the primary egocentric narcissistic phase, but in some cases, the child may behave in this manner chronically because he is suffering from some form of abuse or neglect of his needs.

Narcissistic injury occurs as a result of the messages of parents, relatives, teachers, friends, neighbors, society, and even strangers. No one can totally avoid narcissistic injuries. We all have wants and desires that we cannot get. Our reactions to these narcissistic injuries can be unconsciously arrested at infancy or age two, like the boy with the sneakers. The neural wiring of the brain of this boy maintains the painful experiences in the **hippocampus** (the memory section of the brain). When the brain is wired by repeated actions of neglect or rejection, you can have emotional flashbacks to these memories if you have not learned how to forgive and extract negative emotions. For example, if the younger boy had said, "No! You can't have my sneakers," the fifteen-year-old might have a painful emotional moment, and the pain is the same pain he felt when his mother said

No when he was two years old. Now, however, he can react with a gun.

We all have narcissistic scars that are sitting in the social brain, waiting for a healing, most likely not in the extreme way as the boy who wanted the fancy sneakers. Most individuals are completely unaware that they suffer from neural connections derived from narcissistic injuries that occurred primarily in early childhood and adolescence, but also in adulthood from society or from adult relationships.

Emotional deprivation can result in compensatory narcissistic fantasies and a grandiose sense of self, which arise as forms of self-preservation. These compensatory narcissistic fantasies may lead to a feeling of entitlement, resulting in self-centeredness that is characterized by defensive maneuvers, such as blaming others, blaming society, nursing revenge fantasies, or actually acting aggressively out of a sense of justifiable entitlement. A person who is grandiose and has entitlement rage may seek to overcome feelings of helplessness and powerlessness by mirroring the abusive, non-empathic and cold behaviors of the non-nurturing or neglectful parent or by mirroring the behaviors of a dominant culture that inflicts power through violence and forced oppression (Miller, 1979; Kohut, 1972).

CHARACTERISTICS OF THE COVERT NARCISSIST

- Distrusts others.
- Fears victimization and injustice.
- Has terroristic goals
- Retaliatory rage, which can range from + 1 (angry and upset) to +10 (dangerous).

- May have a history of trauma due to childhood abuse or neglect.
- Fantasizes about taking violent revenge.
- Have copycat behaviors of the abuser.
- Is unable to trust others in positions of authority or power.
- Becomes a warrior with a "save yourself" morality. Many gang leaders who suffer from covert narcissism have a philosophy of, "Never, ever, tolerate abuse." May view the world as a war zone.
- May become a terrorist with a "kill them before they (dominant culture) kill you" attitude.
- Develops inappropriate social skills and exhibits a demeanor of rebellious protest.
- Generally, affect (facial energy) is angry, depressed, distrustful, or threatening.
- Self-medicates (drugs, alcohol, food, sex).
- Due to narcissistic injuries have fears, anxiety, or retaliatory emotions from childhood or adolescence that are largely unconscious.
- Through anger and rage, depletes the happiness neurochemicals of the brain, which leads to drugs, alcohol, nicotine, compulsive overeating, or criminal activities.
- May have identity confusion and a false belief system about the word "Black," in which being Black means being aggressive, being a criminal or a gangster, being bad, or being the black sheep (uneducated, unemployed, a failure).
- May have a history of criminal behaviors.
- May have a history of incarcerations.
- Suffers from social isolation and lost productivity.
- May be depressed and socially phobic.

- Exhibits anti-social behaviors, such as stealing, lying, and bullying.
- Have difficulties with intimacy, love, commitment, and with creating a stable family lifestyle.
- Have financial difficulties.
- Suffers from anxiety and paranoid disorders.
- Seeks attention through self-neglect or creating a bizarre appearance.
- Is codependent. In her book *Codependent No More,* Melody Beattie(1987) defines codependence as allowing another person's pathological behavior (overt narcissism, alcoholism) to affect you to such an extent that a non-alcoholic or non-narcissistic person becomes dysfunctional and cannot effectively care for him/herself. Codependent people become obsessed with the dysfunctional or irresponsible behaviors of others ("These people did this, and these people did that;" or "This person makes it impossible for me to...")." They have a host of terms for being a victim and thus are unable to enhance their own potential and have a successful life (Beattie, 1987).
- Is rigid about the behaviors of others, known as black-and-white thinking.
- May have a history of psychiatric hospitalization.
- Suffers from inherited retaliatory stress and feels entitled to be angry and rageful. Killer rage, or black rage, is passed down from one generation to the next.

DISTINCTIONS BETWEEN OVERT AND COVERT NARCISSISM

A person with covert narcissism may exhibit characteristics that are similar to an individual with overt narcissism. However, prisons and psychiatric hospitals are full of individuals with covert narcissism, which is trauma-linked narcissism. Overt narcissism is driven by desire for self-enhancement, power, and control, whereas covert narcissism is driven by a desire to harm others out of rage and revenge—trauma linked narcissism.

Another difference between overt and covert narcissism is developmental, based on how it was acquired. Overt narcissists' likely wear a smile, received good educations, and did not lack for material things. Most likely, their narcissistic needs were satisfied, but it wasn't enough for them. Overt narcissists practice being disciplined people, seek to be in control, and seek to be viewed as superior and admired. They only become criminals or violent when things do not go the way they want or their egos are threatened in some way (Baumeister, et al, 1993).

Covert narcissists, unlike the overt narcissists, did not grow up with a silver or gold spoon in their mouths. They may have a history of abuse, discrimination, and/or abandonment that led to retaliatory stress, rage and revenge. The covert narcissist is unhappy, fearful, distrustful, anxious, and angry, and retaliation becomes a way of life.

CHAPTER 4

RETALIATORY STRESS DISORDER, ENEMY-MEMORY, RAGE, & CRIMINAL BEHAVIORS

Retaliatory stress disorder (RSD) is a maladaptive bio-socio-psychological disorder often characterized by rageful reactions to being ostracized, oppressed, discriminated against, or victimized in some form. In short, RSD is the angry brain. Some have referred to this type of stress and trauma as enemy-memory. Shelby Steele in his book the *Content of Our Character*, stated that the greatest problem for African Americans related to the magnitude and memory of oppression; and the impact of family destruction with divide and conquer. The memory of horrific past events can be triggered by walking into a store and hearing a strong southern accent. This strong accent could pull the memory forward about oppression. This enemy-memory could lead to an exaggerated reaction of defensiveness towards the person with the southern accent (Steele, 1990).

Enemy-memory can originate from historical or collective memories of past traumatic events, triggering rage and retaliatory behaviors in the present. The impact of enemy-memory is based largely on unconscious information. It can be personal or it can be related to traumatic events of others: parents, grandparents, great-grandparents. It can also be related to the community in which you were born, such as memories of police brutality (Berntsen, & Rubin, 2002). The conscious and unconscious memories of traumatic cultural events related to hate, violence, or past traumas can be factors of retaliatory stress and cultural distrust, and not due to typical delusional paranoia (Whaley, 2001; Whaley, 1998).

The collective social unconscious is our psychic inheritance contains the emotional spirits of our immediate and past ancestors (Boeree, 2009; Farmer, 2014). When there is a history of trauma, the untreated, unconscious social behavior can trigger a memory that leads to killer rage, as in the experience written about in Bell Hooks' book on racism. She is a writer raised in South Africa with an historical memory of apartheid. The area of mental health related to emotions and historical memories, like the story of the lynching of Arthur Steven, is not widely covered or researched, thus, little is known as to how emotional unpleasantness, depression, and traumatic experiences affect mental health relative to the long-term retention of autobiographical memories passed down from one generation to the next (Berntsen & Rubin, 2002).

The hippocampus is the memory area of the brain. If it is flooded with negative thoughts and memories of what others have done—or are doing now—to you or to your family/ancestors, these thoughts may trigger a desire to get revenge and strategies for retaliation. Retaliatory stress is stress, and it can make you physically ill (Talbott, 2002). It is a factor that can lead to cardiovascular disease, hypertension, obesity, type 2 diabetes, sleep disorders, and even cancer. Retaliatory stress can make you mentally ill, leading to cultural distrust that is diagnosed as paranoid thinking, anxiety, depression, and even suicide. RSD will degrade your quality of life. Retaliatory stress is a type of stress that can affect individuals who have a history of victimization. This becomes chronic stress if parents and grandparents were also victimized. Victimization is trauma, and trauma leads to stress, which can lead to mentally and physically dysfunctional behavior if not effectively treated.

Mental health scientists have discovered a relationship among stress, emotions, and behavioral reactions that impact your brain and body chemistry (Amen, 1998). What does this mean? If you are angry because you lost your job due to discrimination, yes, you should be upset and disappointed. Physical reactions to a thought lead to chemical changes in the nervous system and you are hurting yourself if you begin to perseverate on negative thoughts, *"Oh, this person is a racist... I hate... I want to hurt... I'm fed up with this injustice..."* Or you might be thinking, "This injustice also happened to my father, and he lost his job because of racism," or you might be thinking *"My grandfather was in prison because of racism..."* These are your inherited memories, read Butterfield, 1995, to have a better understanding of inherited memories.

Traditional therapy seeks to assess your immediate family history. With social brain healing you go beyond the immediate family history. Your father may not have been in your life. Being angry at him will not bring about emotional healing or spiritual growth or prefrontal cortex (PFC) development, which allows for advance success like becoming an electrical engineer. You must understand the impact of world history and the dynamics of racism and cultural practices of divide and conquer on mental health and on brain development to be fully able to forgive and bring happiness and advance success into your life.

A thought is a mental image and as you dwell on negative thoughts you are building up stress hormones in your mind and body that will negatively affect your emotional mind, causing rage and retaliation. And over time, you will injure your immune system's ability to defend against infections and disease. You are also weakening the ability of your mind and body to process executive functions and logical information in areas of the brain like the prefrontal cortex (PFC), which might have led you to a peaceful solution and the ability to sublimate your actions for positive success.

I had a young African American male client whose mother was fired from her job by a European American boss. A few weeks later, this boy went to school and attacked his European American teacher. In our therapy sessions he stated he was fed-up and angry about the behaviors of racist's people. His PFC was not developed as PFC is not completely developed until later in life. However, after attacking his teacher his life path was special education and psychiatric hospitals. He carried inherited memories of his grandmother and now negative mental images of what was happening to his mother. Subsequently, he was expelled from school. His negative thoughts became thoughts leading to poorly beginning stages of a developed PFC because his mother was fired and inherited memories of racism.

Maybe you contributed to your firing status, were late, had an attitude, and maybe you were distrustful and unfriendly. RSD leads to cognitive distortions that produce inaccurate analysis of a situation. For example, you may not be able to see clearly whether you had a role in your dismissal. Of course, you might have been a perfect employee, always early and kind to your co-workers, and in the world we live in, you could still get fired. You may have been dismissed because of discrimination or racism. Ultimately, in such a situation, you will have to accept what has happened and determine whether there are any legal actions you can take.

When you confront what you may consider dangerous or disturbing, the stress response is to fight or flee. This mechanism has served humans well over the life span of the human race, but the stress response is overworked under the multiple pressures of our modern world. Many of us are in stressed states because of the injustices of the world, like being unfairly fired from a job; a narcissist spouse; as well as traumatic events from childhood, adolescence, and adulthood, which can freeze the fight/flight circuitry. Let's call this frozen circuitry the HPA axis, or simply HPA.

HPA stands for hypothalamus-pituitary-adrenal axis. When the HPA is frozen in fight or flight, it obliterates the mind's ability to say No to aggressive, criminal, and violent behaviors. I have worked for over thirty years with individuals in hospitals, residential facilities, and juvenile settings. When I meet certain people, I can see that they have a frozen HPA. If I become their personal therapist, my goal is to defrost the HPA.

THE CASE OF THE 350-POUND SAFETY NET

At a children's hospital, I was working with a patient who had been transferred from another psychiatric hospital. He was fifteen years old, African American, about six feet tall, and weighed over 350 pounds. For most of his time at the prior children's hospital, he had been mostly in seclusion and restraints. At my hospital, as they were searching for restraints that could fit such a big person, I said, I would take the case and I didn't want to start with any restraints. I met the boy along with his dad when he arrived at the hospital. We sat down and talked. The boy told me he had no desire to lose weight because his weight was his safety net, but he got real angry when peers teased him about it. So, his weight was a double-edged sword. On the one hand, it was protection and on the other hand, it was a trigger.

He learned that criticism and being yelled at were his triggers. Being yelled at or criticized came under the trigger category of "disrespect." Over the course of his treatment, he gained some knowledge of how to cope with anger using a Human skill, which you will learn about later in this book. By doing ancestral regression of past stories of slavery times and stories from his father and grandfather, as well as current stories, he learned why he had spent a year in shackles. After working on acceptance of his world rather than retaliation against it, he was able to see good things about himself and his world. I gave him some social brain healing suggestions and taught him a sign, non-verbal activity that he could use when he felt overwhelmed. I always greeted him with smiles, and over the course of working with me as his primary psychotherapist, he gained the strategies to defrost his HPA and heal his social brain. During his entire stay at the hospital, he did not require any restraints, and he was allowed to return home.

Many individuals develop chronic retaliatory stress symptoms of fight or flight due to acts of discrimination, trauma, or feelings of victimization. In the case of the 350-pound adolescent, he wanted to be big and aggressive so that people would leave him alone, stop calling him gay, and stop victimizing him. He came from a middle-class, intact family, but to be safe, he had to act a certain way to show he had street-bad-boy credits. At his school, he was called gay for speaking intelligently. If he wasn't seen as aggressive, he was called gay. Asian males, he noticed, could be intelligent and non-aggressive, and no one called them gay. He had some personal issues with his family, and he was being teased at school, but his fears were enhanced by the history of victimization related to memories of crimes against slaves and Jim Crow. We could call this the *mentality of victimization,* and it can lead to chronic negative thoughts that freeze the HPA and subsequently lead to impulsive aggressive actions of retaliation.

At age fifteen, he was already needing restraints and being locked in a seclusion room, just like the slaves in the 1600s. This was a boy who had the natural potential to graduate college and positively contribute to our society; instead, he was suffering from RSD and had been isolated like an untamed animal.

A frozen HPA interferes with the higher reasoning part of the brain, the prefrontal cortex (PFC). This brain area takes time to develop; it is not fully matured until young adulthood, approximately ages twenty-three to twenty-seven. The PFC is involved in executive functions, judgment, empathy, and the ability to slow down reactions to painful situations. This mediation center of the brain allows for an inhibitory function, the ability to say no to socially inappropriate behaviors and the ability to say yes to appropriate behaviors. When the PFC is underdeveloped, it cannot do its job to slow down and/or prevent impulsive negative emotional reactions, and these can lead to criminal activity and aggressive reactions.

Scientists have also found a relationship between narcissism and aggression even in children (Barry, Barry, Lochman, Adler & Hill, 2007). When I was a PhD student, my hope was to research the relationship of narcissism, trauma, retaliatory stress, and criminal behaviors in adolescents, like my 350 pound safety net patient, but I was never given the opportunity. Nonetheless, I learned more than I could in a classroom, from working with children like my 350 pound client. He made progress, no more chains of restraints, and he was allowed to return home.

The United States is a great and wonderful country, but we can do more to reduce covert narcissism, retaliatory stress, and improve mental health. Over the years, after working with aggressive individuals, I questioned them to determine if they were prone to grandiose thinking. I developed my own theories around retaliatory stress and narcissism, using my clients who had negative thoughts of retaliation and aggression. I started referring to them as having retaliatory stress disorder (RSD), which means they felt entitled to their aggressive reactions.

Many suffering from RSD have legitimate reasons to be angry and never learned how to transcend the rage due to trauma and enemy-memory. Most treatment methods do not address RSD or enemy-memory, which means that patients like my 350-pound adolescent can spend a lifetime in some form of restraint or prison life, coping with the unconscious and conscious anxiety and rage of victim mentality.

NARCISSISM AND CRIMINAL BEHAVIORS

Retaliatory stress can lead to aggression and criminal behaviors. Scientists have shown that individuals prone to violence are based on their personal beliefs of entitlement and superiority. Such individuals with overt narcissism are prone towards murder, raping, wife beaters, violent gang activity, terrorists and aggressive nations have views of superiority (Baumeister, Bushman & Campbell, 2000). Covert narcissistic individuals with retaliatory stress disorder will resort to violence and criminal behaviors because of a sense of being disrespected or having a sense of wounded pride (Baumeister, et al., 2000). I reviewed a chart of countries with reported high rates of criminal behavior. My hypothesis is that the higher the crime rate, the higher the levels of narcissism, both overt and covert. Based on information from the countries with the highest reported crime rates the United States was the highest of developed countries. See: http://www.mapsofworld.com/world-top-ten/countries-with-highest-reported-crime-rates.html

CASE ILLUSTRATION: THE STORY OF PAT

Pat was a young lady in her twenties. She had a boyfriend whom she had loved for over five years. Pat came from an intact family, went to church regularly, and was a college student. She had never been in trouble at school or in her community. However, in her search for a boyfriend, she was looking for someone hip and a bad-boy type—I guess not like her father, a hard worker who was dedicated to his family. With her hip, bad-boy boyfriend, she was always stressed because he cheated on her and flirted with other women in front of her.

Eventually, she got pregnant without being married or engaged. Pat and her bad-boy boyfriend got an apartment together when their son was born. Pat thought that having a baby would change her bad-boy boyfriend. It didn't. He would stay out and sometimes not return for two or three days. Pat stayed at home with the baby, all alone, ruminating in anger and depleting her natural neurochemicals for happiness. Subsequently, on one early morning when her hip, bad-boy boyfriend returned, Pat destroyed items in the apartment, and then took a knife and stabbed bad boy numerous times. She was arrested and had to stay in jail for a few nights. Pat lost her job, and she was referred to me for court-ordered anger management. She suffered from retaliatory stress disorder (RSD).

CONSEQUENCES OF RSD AND RAGE:

- Unhealthy interpersonal relationships: work, marriage, family.
- Financial distress: rage reactions can lead to physical damages, loss of job.
- Road rage: you can damage your car and even kill others.
- Home rage: you can damage items in your home, which are costly to repair.

If you are spending most of your time thinking about the bad things happening to you and the injustices that you have incurred, you may over time become paranoid, depressed, anxious, or suicidal, leading to poor mental health or negative reactions, as in the case of Pat. It is true that you cannot avoid painful experiences; still, you need to be mindful that painful experiences are a reality in the world we live in. You can take steps to avoid victimization. However, will you avoid it 100 percent? I know I didn't.

Progressively, as you will learn, you can prevent the depletion of the neurochemicals in your social brain; progressively, you can move towards improved mental health and happiness in this imperfect world that we live in prone to hurtful actions. We must progressively find the elements in our world for joy, peace, and happiness. With knowledge you can find that joy.

CHAPTER 5

EMOTIONAL TRAUMATIC BRAIN INJURY (ETBI) — TRAUMA DAMAGES BRAIN CHEMISTRY

I'm sure you have heard about traumatic brain injuries caused by car accidents, infections, cancer, or physical blows to the brain. Humans also experience emotional blows to the brain following emotional stress. Using magnetic resonance imaging (**MRI**), functional magnetic resonance imaging (**FMRI**), positron emission tomography (**PET**), or single photon emission computed tomography (**SPECT**), scientists have discovered that brain structure is impacted not only by physical growth, cognitive experiences, and brain injuries; but that it is also affected by behavior, social interactions, reactions to trauma, emotional maturity, and psycho-social functioning (Amen, 1998). Emotional traumatic brain injury (ETBI) can start in infancy, childhood, adolescence, or adulthood; its effects can last for a lifetime and can be transmitted to the next generation.

As you have learned, I refer to narcissism as a social mental illness. We all went through the narcissistic phase in childhood, some more obviously than others. You learned that when an infant's needs are not met due to abuse or negligence, this can result in damage to the orbitofrontal cortex (OFC) of the brain. You have learned that the two-year-old having temper tantrums when frustrated is due to the child's underdeveloped nervous system. You have learned about the HPA axis and how traumatic events of childhood, adolescence, and adulthood can cause the fight/flight circuitry to become a frozen circuitry.

When the HPA is frozen in fight or flight, the brain is in a state of injury—ETBI, and the mind's ability to say no to aggressive, criminal, and violent behaviors is significantly impaired. Scientists have reported that early traumatic experiences can result from narcissistic parenting and narcissistic neglect or a lack of parental nurturance (Zamostny et al., 1993;Watson, Hickman, & Morris, & Milliron 1995). Narcissistic parents are parents more engaged in their own needs than they are in the needs of their child and/or parents who tell the child that he/she is superior. Narcissistic neglect occurs when parents consider their own needs, such as their drug addiction or alcoholism, more important than the needs of their child. Ego-centered parenting and neglectful parenting are forms of abuse and can alter the brain activity of the child, resulting in cognitive distortions and difficulty in processing information about self and others (Perry, Pollard, Blakley, Baker, & Vigilante, 1996).

You have learned that in a narcissistic culture individuals may and usually do experience trauma and pain, which can lead to retaliatory stress and subsequently to reliance on prescription medication or other self-medication, like alcohol, drug abuse, compulsive overeating, and aggressive or criminal behaviors, all of which depletes happy neurochemicals in the brain and damages the brain chemistry for a peaceful lifestyle.

Studies have shown that if children learn that violence, hatred, and retaliation are the prevailing options for coping with conflicts, these behaviors become normal for them and are viewed as a part of human nature (Arnow, 1995; Perry, 1999). Children in states of retaliation and aggressive reactions are unable to fully advance the future abilities of the **prefrontal cortex** (PFC), also called the executive brain because it mediates decision making and plays a role in goal-directed behaviors. It is also aligned with the **orbitofrontal cortex** (OFC), which plays a role in inhibiting the **amygdala**, the emotional brain. Together, the PFC and the OFC slow down the emotions of the amygdala to avoid emotional brain injury, which can be characterized by aggressive reactions or excessive use of drugs and alcohol (Arden & Linford, 2009).

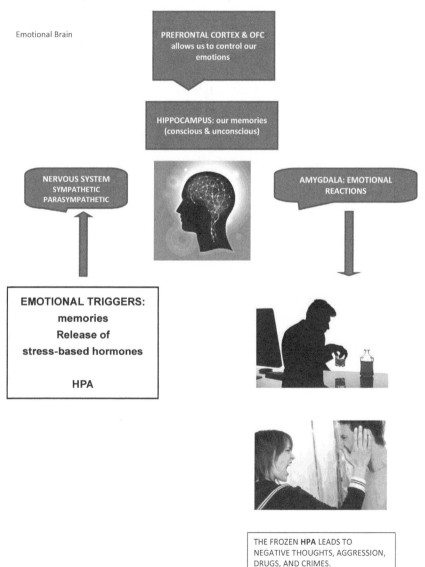

Individuals raised in environmentally healthy settings, free from abuse, neglect, and excessive narcissistic injuries, have more frontal cortex development than individuals raised in deprived settings and exposed to narcissistic injuries. Although PFC is not fully developed until adulthood, what happens in childhood can later impact PFC. If the PFC development is low, and the amygdala system for agitation and fight is high, the individual will be prone to reactive behavior that affects the social brain. The PFC grows with healthy learning, good education, and observations of loving, non-violent relationships between parents, grandparents, friends, teachers, and the larger community.

CHAPTER 6

THE SOCIALIZED BRAIN — HOW THE LABELS BLACK & WHITE CONTRIBUTE TO BELIEFS, THOUGHTS, TRAUMA & VIOLENCE

Words can affect your brain. Your beliefs and thoughts are composed of the words you have heard from birth. Words create neural pathways and can impact the wiring of your brain, how you think, and subsequently your emotional DNA. Your thoughts, ideas, and beliefs are based on what your senses internalize—neurons that fire together, wire together. How you relate to others begins with the relationship between you as an infant and an adult, generally the parent or the caregiver.

The adult is expected to respond to the infant's needs, which are numerous, and in such a way that the child feels secure and appreciated. Much work has been done by social scientists such as Bowlby (1973) and others, who wrote about parenting and attachment. If, during early development, a child receives consistent, positive emotional responsiveness, positive attention, positive words of affirmation, and affection; given with a loving, happy, and smiling face, the child will feel secure (Karen, 1994). This period of interpersonal interactions between the parent and child with words and body actions sets the stage for later PFC brain growth for positive, healthy interactions with others. Negative parenting messages or negative community messages, including those from television, video games, and movies, can have an adverse effect on brain development, which will later interfere with PFC growth and moral decisions (Arden & Linford, 2009).

Trauma that interferes with brain chemistry stems from the messages of your home and your community, causing you to internalize feelings of self-hate through conditioning or by words or labels like *Black*—the black sheep, the black heart, black behavior, black English, a black day, a black soul. Children being told that they are Black can internalize negative beliefs and thoughts about themselves from the label *Black*, and this can lead to brain chemistry that slows down the long-term growth of their PFC and moral system.

Terms like *Black* have historical roots in the English language. For example, I attended a conference led by a European American psychologist who worked with young children. A child who was having a good day would hold up a yellow card; a child who was feeling sad, angry, or upset would hold up a black card.

The word *Black* is a contaminating word, and serves as a stereotype that only confuses the mind or social brain of a young child. It is an English word that comes from the British culture, a culture that historically viewed *Black* as inferior. Black or blackness or darkness in this culture has historically been the common symbol for evil, wickedness, paganism, the devil, death, illness, and the forbidden. It was not uncommon for European artists to portray the tormentors of Christ as Black figures (Hartman & Husband, 1995). The opening scene to Shakespeare's *Othello* portrays the distress of Desdemona's father at the news that his daughter is in the gross clasp of a lascivious Moor. "He is told that an old black ram is tupping his white ewe, and he is convinced that his daughter could not have married a Moor had she been in her right mind, but must have been drugged or bewitched through practices of cunning hell, so to err against all rules of nature" (Hartman & Husband, 1995). Many definitions of blackness predate the African slave trade.

The word *White* is another word stemming from British European culture, but it is the opposite of the word Black. Europeans and European Americans identify with the word *White*, which is the common symbol of goodness, the angelic, master, conqueror, super-strength (superman), wealth, power, beauty, and supremacy given by God. In the popular movie *White Fang*, the star wolf meets a totally all-white wolf. This all-white wolf exhibits behaviors of goodness, love, and kindness. The star wolf also meets an all-black wolf that is a loser and exhibits aggressive and evil behaviors. Children are constantly exposed to such color images; they are mentally programmed for black and white thinking.

It is my opinion that these consistent portrayals of black and white teach children to believe in the evil and aggressiveness of Blackness and the goodness and beauty of Whiteness. We are exposed to this Black-and-White color pollutant every day, and yet we are surprised when Black children choose a white doll over a black doll. Messages a child hears on TV or within the community contributes to brain neural pathways and the arousal of a mental state, which eventually leads to traits. Neurons that fire together wire together. Subsequently, the young child referred to as Black will intrinsically develop a neural pathway whether conscious or unconscious of a belief system that White is better, that White is superior even a superman. He/she may also develop a neural pathway of being a Black sheep, inferior and aggressive.

THE CASE OF MS. JOHNSON

I was teaching parenting skills to a beautiful African American woman, Ms. Johnson. I wanted her to change her way of communicating with her children, especially with her oldest, a thirteen-year-old son, who was my client. She was given the task of not yelling, cursing, or referring to her children as *nigger, bitch,* or saying things like, *"Nigger, get your black ass over here,"* when she was angry with him. She was to minimize criticism, maximize the use of her son's name when talking to him, and find ways of praising him every day (words of affirmation). As an aid, she was given a list of nearly a hundred different ways to praise her son. I asked Ms. Johnson not to exhibit any type of anti-social behaviors in front of her children, such as smoking marijuana or using profanity.

I attempted to use a role-playing method with her so that she could practice new behaviors. At our second session, she yelled at me, "I'm not gonna use this *white* treatment on my son; these are nothing but *white* people ways." I told her I disagreed; I did not feel that praising her children or calling them by their proper names had anything to do with White culture.

Her response was that I was acting *White.* I told her that I disagreed, and that in many ways I felt she was more inclined towards White culture. This disturbed her. She started using a slew of profanity and body gestures to indicate how she follows *Black* culture. I explained to her that the words she was using are the same words that *Whites* used towards *Blacks,* I refer to it as *White rage.* In the 1600s when Blacks in America did not do as they were told they experienced *White rage.* In my analysis of Ms. Johnson she had incorporated into her social brain the words, attitudes and beliefs of the White slave masters.

I read her some quotes from the book, *To Be A Slave,* by Julius Lester.

> *We didn't know nothing like young folks do now. We hardly knowed our names. We was cussed for being so many niggers, bitches, sons of bitches, bloody bitches and blood of bitches. We never heard our names scarcely at all. Slaves were whipped for the most trifling incidents. The master would make us slaves steal from other slave owners.(Lester 1968, p. 29).*

I also read to her an example of an African mother-child relationship before exposure to European slavery culture and *White rage.*

> *When they put us in irons to be sent to our place of confinement in the ship, the men who fastened the irons on these African mothers, took the children out of their hands and threw them over the side of the ship into the water. When this was done, two of the women leaped overboard after their children—the third was already confined by a chain to another woman and could not get into the water, but in struggling to disengage herself, she broke her arm and died a few days later of a fever (Lester, 1968, p. 25).*

After reading the quotes, I told Ms. Johnson I didn't think a mother who would jump overboard to save her baby or to die with her child would find it hard to praise that baby, or to refer to him by his given name. Praising her children and speaking to them in a loving and respectful manner should be little to ask.

All of Ms. Johnson's children had been either in juvenile court, psychiatric hospitals, foster homes, or residential treatment centers. All had states of trauma, a frozen HPA, and an underdeveloped pathway for prefrontal cortex growth. Her kids were failing in school, but she referred to them as ignorant, despite the fact that the intellectual abilities of all her children were within normal limits or higher than normal.

Ms. Johnson was of mixed heritage. Her White heritage had abandoned her, abused her, and told her how horrible her Black father was. He was called all kinds of negative words, and so was Ms. Johnson. Growing up in that negative environment, she had neural brain connections just like those a racist would have. However, she considered those attitudes and language as being a strong Black woman. This made it easy for her to use such words as *nigger* and avoid using praiseful or kind words towards her children. She loves her children, but sees her children as Black, and being Black means the black sheep, the good for nothing. It also means being strong, tough, even aggressive and not taking crap from others.

She was unable to motivate them to be lawyers, doctors, engineers and/or to have successful careers and, later, successful marriages. She was unable to motivate them to see positive things about themselves and about the world they lived in and could contribute to. She was unable to motivate them to be peaceful and non-violent. Ms. Johnson's brain connection was that *Black* was aggressive, uneducated, inferior, and good for nothing; this energy of her brain was passed on to her children. She was making sure that her children were going to be

Black. She rebelled against my approach of loving kindness, hugs, and praises of her children's abilities and non-abilities.

The brain has a negativity bias; the negative words are saved in your memory (the hippocampus) much longer than kind words. The suggestion of using 100 positive praising words to her children daily would have begun the healing for progressive mental health, but Ms. Johnson wanted to raise her kids the *Black* way. Today, a "Black male" label means you are a bad boy, aggressive, street-wise. It rarely means you are an engineer, own a billion-dollar corporation, or invented a new, more effective, vehicle. The word Black is engraved in the unconscious and every association you have heard since birth; it has been etched into your mind. Subsequently, Black becomes a real life self-image. Your inner unconscious monologue is that Black does not own corporations. Black is not a millionaire. Black is not a loving caring father and husband.

I was doing counseling with a couple who had been together for over ten years. The husband worked long hours, and when he was home, he sat and watched a lot of comedy shows and sports. He was an easygoing, responsible person, and he was the one who initiated the couple therapy for himself and his wife. In his first session, he said his wife yelled, cursed, and called him nigger, and he wanted this to change. Most of the time he ignored her, but there were times when he got fed up and reacted with hurtful words to her.

When I met his wife, I saw that she was a strong woman and that she was very critical of her husband. She admitted that she could be loud, but stated, "He met me this way." She also admitted that her husband ignores her most of the time, just sitting in his favorite chair, watching TV, and the only way she could get his attention was through negative attention. When she yells and curses at him, she gets a response.

I developed a plan for them to restructure how they communicate to each other. I told them it was called the imago approach (Hendrix, 1988), had been seen on the Oprah show, and was used widely to help couples communicate better. I let them know that I had been married for nearly twenty-five years and my husband and I used the approach. It works like this:

Let's begin with the wife. She was to ask her husband, "Can I talk to you? Is this a good time?" If they both agree that it is a good time, the person making the request may talk for up to fifteen minutes about something he did that she did not like; or what he could do to make her feel loved and appreciated, but she had to speak in a respectful, calm manner. They practiced the technique in my office and both agreed to use it. They were asked to return in one week. The following week, I asked the wife if she had used the method. Her reply was, "I'm a Black woman, and I don't talk that way. This reminds me of slavery time."

I told her that in the time of slavery, people talked in a "forced subservient" manner. A forced subservient manner is forced respect, and if you didn't use the forced subservient manner, you were lynched or shot dead. Slaves talked in a forced subservient manner so they could live or survive.

"I'm asking you to speak in a respectful and kind manner to your husband because you made a vow to love, honor, and respect him. I'm asking you to talk in a respectful manner because if you yell, curse, and call your husband degrading names, it's unlikely that anyone will lynch you, but your behavior is traumatizing and creating feelings of anger in your husband.

In this case, the wife's sense of self was being Black, which meant she could yell, scream, curse, and refer to her husband as nigger when he angered her. I told them of a time when I was teaching at a business college. I often stayed up late preparing lesson plans so I could teach in a way that would enable my students to learn the materials and do well on their tests. One day, an African American female student said "You treat us like slaves, work, work, work. As soon as we walk into the class, you have an assignment on the board, and you walk around to see what we are doing on our computers." I corrected the student "I walk around to see if anyone needs help with the assignment."

My point in telling the couple of this example was that *being Black* is not related to being successful, working hard to earn As in your course work; it is related to your psychic inheritance of the suffering of the Black community, which is geared towards anger, vengeance, and rage; but expressed as old fashioned white rage or the rage of the master; leading to failure in love and work. This type of anger, vengeance, and rage interferes with peace and happiness or goals for financial success or relationship success.

My student felt she was made to work too hard; so she did not do the hard work. Maybe she has an ancestor who was forced to work too hard. To her, hard work was akin to being a slave, and she subsequently failed the course or was given a poor grade. The ancestral karma related to working hard and slavery had not been resolved in her social brain. The wife felt that talking to her husband in a respectful and kind manner was akin to being a submissive slave and declared she would not change. The marriage ultimately failed, and the ancestral karma related to being respectful, humble, and slavery had not been resolved in her social brain.

The wife was highly resistant to doing a DNA extraction related to the stereotype of being Black, which is a guided-imagery technique, a visualization of *white* rage and the slave oppressive community within. The process includes extracting the words and behaviors used in the slave community, words like Nigger or exhibiting behaviors leading to failing in school or in a relationship. For this wife and my student, working hard was not being Black; being respectful and using loving words of affirmation was not being Black; problem solving of conflicts using calmness, and loving kindness approaches conflicted with their sense of self as being Black.

My client Joyce is a lovely African American lady who entered therapy because of anxiety attacks. She was an attractive forty-year-old female who had never been married. Her speech was full of profanity and slang. One day, she entered therapy very upset with her boss; every other word she spoke was a profanity. I pointed this out, and she stated, "Well, I talk Black, and you talk White." I said a few words in an African language I knew and explained that if she wanted to talk Black, she should learn an African language, perhaps even visit that African country, and then she could claim, "I'm talking Black," or better yet, you can say, "I speak an African language."

I explained that I speak English, which is a European language. I told her that my parents, grandparents, and great-grandparents were born in the United States and, unfortunately, English is the only language I know fluently. "I don't consider it talking White," I said, "but as speaking the English language."

Over the course of her treatment, Joyce was able to reprogram her brain. She began to just speak English, without the rage and profanity. She practiced and was able to incorporate forgiveness, using techniques of ancestral regression, and other methods that you will learn about later in this book. Her anxiety attacks significantly decreased as she became less self-centered and less of an angry-covert narcissist. She also learned that many of her emotional responses are heritable based on the long history of white-and-black labeling. Meanwhile, with therapy, she met a respectable man, and by the end of her treatment, she was engaged and at peace with the world.

Being Black has an intrinsic impact on the brain and one's long-term way of thinking and behaving. This thought of being black, led one African American adolescent girl, who was adopted and raised by European Americans, to become a member of a gang of African Americans for the sole purpose of being Black. In her efforts to be Black she killed a man and ended up in prison (this was a true story taken from the TV show Investigation Discovery). This thought of being Black becomes an external attitude with strong emotional energy to represent being Black, with the mirrored meaning of being a failure in school (the black sheep), using drugs, and being gangster.

CHAPTER 7

THE HEALING PROCESS

Grant me the serenity to accept what I cannot change (other people, or the past); I need courage to change the things I can (myself); and I need to use wise mind to know the difference. Grant me growth of the wise mind/brain beyond the emotional mind/brain of childhood and narcissistic injuries, and beyond the rational/entitled mind/brain of justification which comes with adolescence and young adulthood. Healing starts with knowing that the brain is not hardwired and it can change for peace and success. But you must do the work. (Boza interpretation for healing based on the Serenity Prayer, by Reinhold Niebuhr)

THE CASE OF JOHN

John, age fifteen, had an extensive history of aggressive reactions whenever he feels disrespected. He's been living in a psychiatric hospital since age eleven because he cannot be managed in the community. He is well-groomed, outgoing, and likable, and he has future plans to be a famous hip hop entertainer. He has a long history of aggression toward others, including his medical doctor, whom John gave a black eye after the doctor criticized his behavior. John has bitten staff, perforating the skin. When angry, he has destroyed an entire office. He's been on nearly every medication—antipsychotic, mood disorder, anti-depression, antianxiety, and stimulants, yet he continues to be out of control.

This is an example of John's social information processing; based on steps created by Crick & Dodge, (1996). We all have ways that we process information. You can also use these steps to see how you process information when feeling angry versus when feeling happy. These steps of social information processing that John will use in this illustration are based on the neural pathways in his social emotional brain, which determines how he resolves a conflict. This conflict takes place in a hospital where John is a patient.

A childcare worker tells John that he needs to clean up his room. Following directions is a skill taught at the hospital, and John is cleaning his room. However, after twenty minutes, another staff member arrives and tells John, "It's time for the morning group meeting. Get to the meeting, now."

Step 1: John encodes *externally* that the staff is wrong to ask him to go to the group when another staff told him to clean up his room. John knows that all patients and staff are required to attend morning community meetings. From the staff's tone, John *internally* encodes a threat to his ego, which results in upset feelings and dysregulation (narcissistic injury from an unconscious past event, a past neural synapse). Subsequently, John tries to ignore staff member #2 in an attempt at self-control. Staff member #2 raises his voice again, telling John he needs to write down two hundred negative points for "not following directions," the standard corrective action.

Step 2: John ascribes intent (the brain seeks to describe what is happening; but there can be cognitive distortions) and tries to interpret staff member #2's intent from cues: he is *yelling at me, disrespecting me, and giving me negative points, which I don't deserve because I'm cleaning my room.*

Step 3: John reassesses what he is doing; he is cleaning up his room, which in John's mind is a good thing. He is not bothering anyone, and he is doing what staff member #1 told him to do (clarifying his behavior in his mind). He may even say, "Staff told me to clean up." Staff member #2 insists that it's time for the group meeting, but John must write down his two hundred negative points before going to the group. John has interpreted staff member #2's behavior as "disrespecting him." This is a narcissistic insult John feels insulted and thinks "I insist upon getting the respect that is due me." John, who has a frozen HPA, is simply unable to control his social emotional mind. His interpretation of what is happening between him and staff #2 triggers his neural brain value system as related to DISRESPECT.

Step 4: Subsequently, John constructs a response based on his level of sensitivity. A frozen HPA means the highest level of sensitivity. John sees a book on his bed and generates the idea of throwing it at the perceived provocateur-staff #2. John feels justified in this decision (justified reaction of the social brain) because there isn't a PFC pathway to slow down and reframe his thinking.

Step 5: John retrieves the book and throws it at staff member #2 (enacting his decision); other staff members have already been alerted by a quiet alarm, and they all move to restrain John. When staff member #1 puts his hands on John; John curses at him and bites him deeply, breaking the skin (brain has disassociated from the reality of the situation).

This sequence of social processing emotional information kept John locked up for many years without any progress. John's temperament was NOT hateful, envious, or greed. Rather John's social processing of emotional information was rooted in a neural pathway of distrust and trauma-linked narcissistic traits.

According to Sherwood (1990), individuals with trauma-linked narcissistic traits continue to display this retaliatory problem-solving sequence. The narcissistic traits impede any desire to listen to or accept negative feedback. Thus, this social processing of emotional information sequence, characterized by narcissistic resistance, interferes with social change moving in a more positive direction. Subsequently, adolescents like John remain locked up for years because there aren't any clear, new visions for effective treatment approaches that are geared to reducing or eliminating aggressive reactions using social brain healing techniques geared towards narcissistic resistance.

Adolescents like John struggle with anger and hostility when they receive negative feedback, things don't go their way, someone says NO or criticism, which is often viewed as a verbal attack. In a study by Kernis and Sun (1994), examining the concept of "high unstable self-esteem," it was determined that when individuals with high unstable self-esteem were given negative feedback that could be helpful, they viewed this feedback as incorrect and turned against the evaluator with reactions of anger and hostility. However, when feedback was false but positive, for example getting an A on an essay that should have been rated as a C or less, they rated this feedback as highly credible and the evaluator as highly credible and likable.

The social brain has applications (APPs) of neural determinants that affect the neurotransmitters (chemical energies) in the brain, based on life experiences. In addition, the life experiences of our ancestors APPs contributed to the dynamics of the neurology of the brain. The social brain is based on the degree of use of a faculty. If someone develops a faculty or ability for learning to play piano, there will exist in the brain a space or a neural synapse for piano playing. If the experiences of life program the brain to be angry or to lack empathy towards others, then the brain makes a space or neural synapses for reactive anger and a space to hurt others and not care. We all have a space to react with anger from upsetting life experiences. An infant will yell and scream if not fed: that's anger.

With maturity and PFC development the reactions of anger in the form of yelling, screaming, or hitting become less. We can create neural connections that allow us to cope peacefully with disappointments and conflicts. The brain becomes better able to modulate stressful situations across different social contexts. When the pathways for PFC development are weak, for example, John knew that there was a group meeting with all the patients at nine a.m. every day; but he operated out of his angry brain not a wise mind.

When group time was called, patients stopped cleaning or doing whatever they were doing. Obviously, John did not want to go to group that day; he even preferred cleaning his room. John also knew the steps to the skill for following directions. The steps for following directions were taught to all the patients as a skill for survival, especially when dealing with authority figures, such as police officers, teachers, supervisors, staff members.

- Look at the staff person who is giving the direction
- Say, "Okay," in a calm tone.
- Don't disagree or argue at that time. Just follow the instruction.

- Take a deep breath, smile a half smile, and think, "May I be happy," "May this person be happy."
- Bring up your disagreement with your therapist or, if you are in the community, talk to someone you trust.

Many individuals, especially those with a social unconscious that contains enemy-memory, will have a difficult time learning this skill. The Japanese handled their enemy-memory in many ways, as I have and will advocate in this book. When the Japanese came to the United States several decades ago, they were picked on, called names, and harassed. Whether they were responding to authority or to peers, their responses were humble. The Asian's focus was on education and financial independence, not retaliation. Subsequently, they improved their PFCs.

Humble behaviors can stimulate a brain cortex to withstand the demands of a hostile environment (Huther, 2004). John learned by practicing this skill of following directions via psychodrama and daily recital of the skill. He learned that a police officer who approaches you in a disrespectful manner may have his own psychological issues, may have an inborn temperament to hate or an inborn temperament of xenophobia, which has not been treated.

John learned that it is not his job to teach adults or others a lesson about respect. Just follow directions and be humble in the presence of authority. The act of being humble strengthens the intelligence of the brain (Huther, 2004).

Later, I will teach you to use the Dr. Martin Luther King skill of being humble, like John was able to do. First, though, become trauma-informed about yourself; understand the realities of the world you live in, that everyone in authority (parents, teachers, boss, police) is not respectful, and some have the social mental illness of narcissism, some have inborn temperaments for hate and for xenophobia. Accepting this reality that you have no control over will help you cultivate this skill of following directions, e.g. in your workplace, and rely on giving a more humble response, in the end you benefit and your brain becomes intelligent.

CHAPTER 8

SOCIAL BRAIN HEALING — FIVE PRINCIPLES OF THE REALITY OF THE WORLD

To begin the healing process, you the reader must first acknowledge your hurts and traumas; you must be trauma-informed. You first must acknowledge the hurts of the (a) child within, (b) the mother within, (c) the father within, and (d) your community within, such as friends, your school, your neighborhood, your co-workers, and your country.

When I first started working with John, the boy from the previous chapter, his prognosis was bleak; he was on track to age out of the children's hospital and move into an adult psychiatric institution. I worked with him on the five reality principles below.

THE 1ST PRINCIPLE OF REALITY: KNOW YOUR INNER FACTORS

Construct a trauma-informed list. You cannot heal what you do not recognize. Know your triggers. What truly upsets you? The 1st principle acknowledges that we all get upset and we all have inner factors.

John's list of traumas

- Childhood: Mother's substance abuse, father's abandonment, caregiver's yelling and cursing, death of his closest friend

- Foster Care: Placed in foster care because grandparents had issues of substance abuse and neglect towards their children, his mother.
- Inherited psychic trauma from parents and grandparents
- Enemy-memory

John's dysfunctional emotional style

- Fights with staff and peers
- Black-and-white thinking
- Lacks motivation for an education
- Crimes against others: stealing, destruction of property, seeking street credits
- Retaliatory Stress Disorder
- Low PFC development
- Frozen HPA

John's triggers

- Disrespect
- Criticism
- Authority telling him what to do
- Inconsistency by caregivers e.g. parent not showing up for a visit.
- Issues related to abandonment e.g. lack of love in his life.

John's strengths

- Good verbal ability
- Average intelligence
- Likable
- Some ability to show empathy towards others
- Willingness to participate in the therapeutic process

THE 2ND PRINCIPLE OF REALITY: DON'T JUDGE A BOOK BY ITS COVER

According to Robert Kiyosaki, co-author of *Midas Touch*, the biggest con-artist you may meet often appear to be honest and are well-educated; Mr. Kiyosaki was hurt when he was left holding the bag from such individuals costing him nearly a million in debt (Kiyosaki & Trump, 2011, p 15). Con artist can be attractive, hold advanced degrees, and high positions of leadership. Many are wealthy and will never be arrested or convicted of any crimes or wrongdoing. Why? Because in our society, we have a tendency to view rich, beautiful people in powerful positions almost like gods. We believe what they believe about themselves: that they are perfect people, that they are the smartest. This may be why such individuals rarely go to prison. Some people can steal millions, but they do not represent the criminal population discussed in Chapter 4, if you visited the website: http://www.mapsofworld.com/world-top-ten/countries-with-highest-reported-crime-rates.html. Dr. Kagan's book *The Temperamental Thread: How genes, culture, time and luck make us who we are*, indicates that some individuals have genes or inborn temperament to oppress, bully, and hurt others. Thus, the 2nd principle of reality for the world you live in is not to judge a book by its cover.

External factors are not validation of moral character and empathic ability. Individuals with overt narcissism seek to be admired. Externally, they have proper manners, and they are vain and ego-centered in the extreme, but you cannot tell just by looking at the cover. Many people are xenophobic, but you cannot tell this by external factors. A xenophobic person will not be kind and caring to people they view as different.

Please know that there are many people who are beautiful, wealthy, successful and in fields that require them to promote and market themselves, and at times to be critical of others like Heidi Klum, famous model and host of television show Project Runway and her partner Tim Gunn, these are two beautiful, famous, and rich people who have qualities of humbleness and love of others. It is not their external factors, what you see on the outside that determines who they truly are as a member of the humanoid family. I have never met either Ms. Klum or Mr. Gunn but their positive and caring behaviors on TV contribute to our human family not by external factors but by something internal, loving kindness, which you will learn more about.

Individuals with covert narcissism are also ego-centered in the extreme, but their social illness is almost always more obvious, externally. Thus, the famous two phases: individuals with overt narcissism do at times get caught and go to prison. When that happens people will say oh he doesn't look like a criminal or how such an innocent face could have done such a thing; or these things don't happen in our rich community. Often times many with overt narcissism will say or have a scheme that says "*it was a Black man who did the crime*". For years this was the absolute guaranteed alibi for many overt narcissists. The covert narcissist looks like a criminal. They are prone to daily reactions of rage and revenge thinking, many have frozen HPAs, and their narcissism is trauma-linked. However, like John, many with covert narcissism can be treated with social brain healing, cognitive therapies, and ancestral regression.

John had to become aware of his own ego-centered tendencies; lacking a diagnosis of narcissism as a personality structure, an individual remains resistant to any effort for change (Sherwood, 1990). Diagnosing someone like John with Conduct Disorder or Sociopath has led many therapists to state, "Nothing works." There are narcissists that may be untreatable (Kernberg, 2007). But, John was not untreatable. Unfortunately, my treatment with him was short-term. He was the basis for my research project, which was never approved. Nonetheless, in the short term he was able to be discharged and returned to his community and his family.

What John learned

- Do not judge a book by its cover.
- Know that others may judge you by your cover; you have no control over that; accept it with serenity.
- A teacher may be fair or not fair—resist seeking revenge.
- A peer may not like you—resist fighting back.
- A peer may call you a name—resist fighting back.
- Being Black does not mean you have to physically hurt someone who criticizes you. Being Black does not mean that you avoid advancing your education to increase your bad-boy image. Resist the "book covers" and definitions of *Black.*
- How to process trauma using a world view geared towards transcending his stereotyped false-self view.

THE 3ᴿᴰ PRINCIPLE OF REALITY: WE ALL HAVE ANTS

Dr. Daniel G. Amen is a neuroscientist and psychiatrist. In his book, *Change Your Brain, Change Your Life* (1998), he refers to negative thoughts as ANTS (automatic negative thoughts). You already know that the brain has a negativity bias and is more sensitive to the negative events that occur in our lives. We all have ANTS. They are just sitting in our brains, mostly unconscious ANTS, but many conscious, as well. Some of us have ANTS that come from our parents' generation and our grandparents' generation. To begin a peaceful life of joy, happiness, and better physical and mental health, you need daily practices to exterminate your ANTS.

What John did to clear out his ANTS

John saw positive mental health and happiness as a new skill he was learning like learning to play the violin. John learned that his angry aggressive behaviors blocked his happy and kindness neurochemicals from being released into his body and mind. John had to practice to create this new neutral pathway for positive mental health. John began with five positive affirmations that I encouraged him to think about and to be grateful for every day. Over time, we increased the positive affirmations. He also built up a resistance to narcissistic injuries when teachers were unkind, peers said hurtful words, or caregivers ignored him.

You can gain control over your emotional mind by eliminating as many ANTS as possible; this is one type of DNA extraction. I got rid of the ANTS related to my online university experience by reframing what happened to me and thinking about what I am grateful for from that bad experience. For one thing, it helped me to write this book. I spent over ten years researching narcissism, aggression, xenophobia, trauma, as well as studying about the first humans and totemism, which is kinship with all life form, and you will learn about totemism later in this book. With my clients, my bad experiences help me to help them reframe their stories of pain and take control over their emotional responses. Changing how you handle your bad experiences can help to stop abusing your body with drugs, alcohol, food, or increasing negative angry hormones, which impact the immune system. My researching, reading, and studying neuropsychology helped me to create a concept of social brain healing and learn more how ANTS deplete your happy-brain neurochemicals, which consequently will negatively impact physical and mental health.

THE 4TH PRINCIPLE OF REALITY: WE NEED GOALS

We are all visitors to the planet. No one owns the planet, we are here to visit and contribute for loving kindness not for hate, violence and rage. For some humans it is a short visit and others have a fairly long visit. Your visit requires that you have a purpose for your life and make goals for yourself. One early goal that many of us may struggle with is to learn to outgrow and transcend the narcissistic reactions of the two-year-old *within* when you don't get your way or when people say No or reject you. Don't spend your visit here on Earth fighting with others because things did not go your way. Practice narcissistic resistance, just like fifteen-year-old John had to do. You can strengthen your resilience to the toxic behaviors of others if you have goals for success and use the principles of this 4th reality to contribute positive energy to the planet.

My first questions to John were: What is important to you? What do you want from this life? He truly wanted to live in the community with his family; he had siblings. He did not know his biological father, and maternal rights had been removed from his biological mother. He also wanted to develop his PFC; in his words, "I want to study and be a good student and one day be able to work or write music."

John was able to set goals for himself so that he could successfully live in his community. He had never been able to manage himself outside of the hospital for more than a few hours because he would get mad and become violent, destroying property or striking out at people. He was a big, strong guy, and he walked around with an angry look. I told him that going home was possible, but to do so, he would have to set a goal of maintaining a positive attitude and practice narcissistic resistance.

Negative thinking is a goal for someone who wants to live in an institution, especially if you are a poor person. People you see on TV with negative thinking are being paid and getting rich. If you are not getting paid millions for being a bully or fighter like Mike Tyson, I suggest you create a goal to decrease your negative thinking, and not emulate TV behaviors. Negativity leads to depletion of happy neurochemicals and poor physical and mental health. Negativity can lead to aggression, substance abuse, obesity, and poor mental health. The brain is prone to negative thinking and negative reactions, so John made goals for positive thinking. I used an attention training method called mindfulness. Mindfulness is absolute attention, a humanoid ability to have awareness of the present. John had to be mindful of doing positive behaviors and not doing negative behaviors. He had to do some simple tasks that were geared to disrupting negative energy and moving towards social brain healing. Scientists have shown that it is important of mindfulness in order to begin the healing process for peace, loving kindness and rejuvenation (Altman, 2011). Below is a version of John's first week assignment:

- Every day he must make up his bed as soon as he got out of it, keep his area clean and uncluttered, take a shower when instructed by staff, and keep his hair cut short.
- He had to say quietly a modified version of the Serenity Prayer, take three deep breaths in and very slowing breathe out, and then think of five things to be grateful for, smiling while thinking of those good things.

- He had to be mindful that everyone is not kind, and that's the reality of the way the world is. If he has an unkind teacher, it is not his responsibility to change that person by his negative reactions.

- He had to walk to the hospital school independently, and while sitting in his classroom, he had to think with a half-smile, "I'm happy I can walk to a classroom, I'm happy I can see, I'm happy I can hear what a teacher says."

- He could not use any profanity. This was the most important objective for his first week. And he had to find ways to be kind to others. Saying thank you; saying hello with a smile is kindness and spreads positive energy.

- He had to be willing to resist willfulness-pigheadedness; my way or no way.

Within two months, John had his hair cut short, he asked to wear a tie, got a job at the hospital, and was rated outstanding for his high level of positive customer service. Some of you may not see how these tasks are connected to aggressive behaviors. Science has revealed that you can rewire your mind simply by your thoughts and actions. When John's thoughts and actions changed his brain began to fire and wire on neural pathways for calmness, happiness, and using wise mind. You can start your own social brain healing today by simply following these five tasks for thirty days.

1. Remove clutter from your home and office.

2. Sit quietly and mediate on things you can be grateful for: if you can walk, that's something to be grateful for; if you can see, that's something to be grateful for; if you can sing, that's something to be grateful for; if you have a friend, that's

something to be grateful for. If you can read this book, that's something to be grateful for. Smile about the thing or things you are grateful for.

3. Accept the world you live in and know that you are a part of a human family. Some people do evil, hateful things. But many people do good, loving things. Make the choice not to be hateful or rageful. Say hello and thank you with kindness, spread positive energy throughout your day.

4. Do not try to change others by using aggressive negative reactions. It is not your responsibility to change other people; it is hard enough changing ourselves. If you say hello to someone who doesn't respond back; that's okay, that's the world we live in. Say to yourself *"may this person be happy."*

5. Do not use profanity for 30 days, and then make it a rare event.

Social brain healing starts with increasing the happy hormones in your brain by changing how you think. If you are stressed out, angry, cursing, and focused on the negative behaviors of others whom you have *no* control over, you are depleting and blocking your happy hormones and are at risk for depression, anxiety, and even rage. You are also increasing unhealthy chemicals in your body, such as cortisol, which weakens your immune system and puts you at risk for self-medicating with excessive drugs, alcohol, and food, thus weakening your physical health. Remember, thoughts trigger chemicals in your body: you can have thoughts that heal and bring happiness; or you can have thoughts that lead to pain and suffering; and you can have thoughts that hurt others. Let's aim for thoughts that heal.

You need courage to change who you are when you set positive-thinking goals for yourself. Making positive changes is the right thing for your brain's neural connections (Arden 2010). You can see what drastic changes John was able to make within a short time.

THE 5ᵀᴴ PRINCIPLE OF REALITY: PROTECTIVE CONCERN

Protective concern means developing a realistic way of protecting yourself from the debilitating effects of the invisible cloud of the social mental illness of narcissism. It starts with being aware of narcissism. For example, we had to become aware of road rage and protect ourselves by taking steps to drive defensively for safety rather than with aggressive reactivity. We also had to become aware of AIDS and use protection with partners. There are no BEWARE signs when it comes to narcissism, but you now know some of the personality traits. With protective concern you can have new ways to protect your social brain; you can be happy.

Here are three ways to develop the armor of protective concern

1. Progressive mental health: You need to be able to work. If you are a child, your work is being able to get good grades in school, challenging yourself, and being the best that you can be. Education is work that prepares the brain for progressive mental health. Education allows you to develop your PFC.

2. Financial independence: Develop a skill. You must be able to take care of yourself. Independence comes with education, a skill, a talent and self-care. And you are never too old for an education. I've met 70 year old students.

3. Good physical health: This will be a side-effect of progressive mental health, financial independence, and having thoughts that heal the body and mind. The more happy and calming hormones you can produce and the more you can decrease ANTS, the better your health will be. My mother is ninety-four years old. She is such a calm person. She rarely gets sick, I've never heard her use profanity; she lives on her own, and sees the positive aspects of life. Her biggest ANTS, *"I can't do what I did when I was eighty-five years old."*

CHAPTER 9

DNA EXTRACTION & HAPPY NEURAL PATHWAYS OF THE FIRST HUMANS

Clearly, humans have the DNA (deoxyribonucleic acid) to be violently aggressive and hate others; but just as we have the DNA to learn to read English, do math, build planes and tall buildings, and heal physical illnesses, we also have the DNA to build a loving, caring, kind, and non-violent world by learning ways to extract the DNA of hate, xenophobia and violence by healing the angry brain and changing ancestral karma.

During the summer of 1980, I walked into an emergency room of Mt. Sinai hospital in New York City. I was about six or seven months pregnant at the time. Unknown to me at the time, I had a condition called *irritable bowel syndrome,* which I did not learn about until some years later. This condition worsened during pregnancy and I was having some complications. The doctors in the emergency room stated that I needed a surgical process which required suturing my cervix. After this process, I was told I was fine and could return to work. I returned to work, and within a week or so, the sutures broke and I was back at the hospital. This time I was told about a medication that had helped other females go full-term in their pregnancies and that the medication would not have any negative effect on my baby. The medication is from the labs of Schering Plough Pharmacies, and the name is *Hyperstat I.V.* (diazoxide). This medication was given to me intravenously while I was six - seven months pregnant and administered two or three times. It was administered at high dosages.

Unfortunately, the medication was not able to prevent my son from being born prematurely at six – seven months, as the doctors claimed it would. He was premature weighting 2 pounds 3ounces and remained in the hospital from August 1980 to November 1980. By the time he was two years old, he was diagnosed with mild cerebral palsy, attention deficit hyperactivity disorder, developmental disorder, autism, and profound deafness. At age two he was seen by a medical doctor who specialized in treatment of attention deficit hyperactivity disorders. While waiting to be seen, the doctor came out and said how my son's hyperactive level was beyond anything he had seen before. At age two he was started on medication. I learned that the medication *Hyperstat,* caused birth defects when used on animals, and in adults caused problems in the ear and temporary hearing loss. This adverse reaction affecting the hearing of adults would be proportionately far more violent in its effect on the fragile hearing mechanism of a developing fetus.

The medication was also known to produce fetal or neonatal Hyperbilirubinemia when given to the mother prior to delivery. Hyperbilirubinemia can be a factor in autism and brain damage. I had a law suit, but I lost. The jury I was assigned did *not* have an African American and I did not consider it a jury of my peers. My lawyers who were friends with the lawyers of the pharmaceutical company, Schering Plough, did not show up in court; instead, they sent a young man just out of law school to represent me. My lawyers did not do an adequate job in representing me in this case. After we lost, my lawyers would not appeal. When I asked why they had made such a decision, I was told that the thinking of the jurors was that my son's problems were due to genetics, and not to the medication. Years later, my son and I did DNA testing and discovered that we are not genetically predisposed for any of the conditions with which he was diagnosed. During the trial, the defense attorney stated, "*It was necessary to test medications.*" The implication was clear: hurt some for the larger good.

Because of my son's problems and my failure to win his case against Schering Plough and Mt. Sinai Hospital, I started researching the brain. My thinking was that the medication **Hyperstat** had impacted my son's brain. I knew of several people who had premature babies, and all had turned out to be perfectly normal. The one thing I learned was that there was much about the brain that I did not know.

My main goals for my son were that he:

- Gain control over his behavior
- Show signs of happiness
- Not be an angry person, seeking retaliation
- Would never be criminally arrested
- Would obtain at least an associate's degree from a reputable college
- Would be able to drive a car

Using what you will learn in this chapter and what I learned about the brain, I was able to help my son achieve all six of the goals. Remember it is the humble, kind, and loving brain that leads to real intelligence, emotional intelligence. It is the narcissistic brain and the angry brain that are like volcanos spreading hate, violence, and rage. You can achieve your goals and become a part of the solution for ending rage by using what you will learn.

Neuroplasticity of the brain is what allows us the ability to change our brains (Badenoch, 2008). Neuroplasticity informs us that the brain is not hard-wired (Arden, 2010).). Neuroplasticity informs us that we can do a DNA extraction of negative neural synapses deposited by our parents, past lives of grandparents, caregivers, society, social media, TV, labels like black and white, and our own negative thoughts. DNA has numerous functions. Science is only being to unravel its story. But for this book, think of DNA as data storage areas collecting new information, but keeping the old. In these storage areas you have thoughts, experiences, and behaviors that change the neurochemicals in the brain (Hanson, 2011). A neurodynamic module such as the OFC (orbitofrontal cortex) regulates emotional dynamics (Schore, 2001) by maintaining connections to the limbic structures, and the amygdala, which lead to emotional reactions. The OFC is also involved with the hippocampus, your memory system. Emotional and physical trauma may impact the OFC, subsequently interfering with the brain's ability to regulate behavior. The brain is an extraordinary cellular network that can actually improve and change your level of fitness (Arden & Linford, 2009). Failure to extract leads to repeated bouts of traumatized negative thinking due to bad things happening to you, which decreases your emotional fitness.

Picture having two types of channels within you, negative and positive: the negativity channels deplete your neurochemicals, which makes you physically and mentally sick. The positive channels boost your energy, improve your fitness level for health, and bring you joy, happiness, and love. You can learn to switch from a negative channel to a positive channel. Numerous books have been written about the brain and the body connection (see Amen, 2010; Arden, 2010) that support this claim. Change your thinking by switching off the negative channels and creating new channels in the brain that promote happiness, financial success, and improved mental and physical health.

The goals I set for my clients are for them to learn about their history with the negative channels and learn and practice the development of the positive channels. In other words, they are to increase the number of positive neural connections. This is achieved by finding ways to keep the positive channels active and decrease their use of the negative neural connection channels. Many of us seek to improve our physical health, but we rarely think about what exercises we can do to improve our mental health. When aiming for physical health, you need to focus on diet, exercise, hydration, and self-discipline. When aiming for mental health, you need to (1) rehabilitate your neural synapses to develop a progressive focus on showing loving kindness towards yourself and others; (2) achieving goals for success, (3) extinguishing your own vulnerable narcissistic ego and (4) being aware for your own self-protection that social mental illnesses exists. Being aware, but not being chronically angry for things you have no control over.

TIPS FOR EXTRACTION OF NEGATIVE EMOTIONS WITH THE FOUR HAPPY HORMONES

Here are some tips for extraction of the negativity bias, which the brain is prone towards and difficult to erase without practice. Remember your thoughts and emotions wire your brain for health or dysfunction. These tips are for healing the social brain for the sake of progressive mental health and happiness. You can use these tips and stop your excessive use of alcohol, drugs, food or nicotine. When the neurobiology of the brain is on the channel of anger and rage you will seek some form of relief or treatment. The happy hormones are: **Oxytocin, Dopamine, Serotonin,** and **Endorphin** and can provide relief when coping with the stressors of life. The hormone cortisol is released when you are angry or highly stressed. Cortisol impacts your immune system, thus, also impacting your physical health (Talbott, 2002).

1. Smile and laugh for happy hormones:

Every morning when you get up, take a few minutes to think about what you can be happy for or grateful for. Listen to a radio show like the *Steve Harvey Show* for laughter and entertainment. Laughing and smiling are very healing for your social brain.

John, who had no parents and had been in institutions most of his life, he began to smile about his ability to hear and subsequently communicate and learn. He also came up with four other things to be grateful for. Being grateful is not enough, though—you must smile. Smiling and laughing produce happy hormones in the brain, such as endorphins, and lowers the stress hormones, such as cortisol. Too much cortisol in your body hurts your immune system and, subsequently, hurts your physical and mental health. John was a tough guy, but he was able to process and develop compassion for himself and notice what he could be grateful for. Let's say your partner is criticizing you, calling you names, and cursing at you. You need to increase those neurochemicals in your brain so you can heal and strengthen your resilience. Your partner might have the social illness of narcissism. So, start smiling and doing what you can to heal your brain with happy hormones. Stay away from the angry, retaliatory stress hormones that will deplete your immune system and put you at risk for mental and physical illness.

2. Sit quietly, meditate, and think of things to be grateful for (happy hormones)

No matter where you are, you can take a moment to let the brain have a rest. Breathe in the sunlight and get your Vitamin D. This is how you keep your happy hormones, such as serotonin, alive. Meditation activates the parasympathetic nervous system which allows you to transform and reprogram your brain for peace and humbleness. Take a yoga class. Don't judge yourself if you cannot do all the poses. Just go as often as you can and do the best that you can. Do not be late to the class.

3. Reprogram your brain with music.

Ancient Africans made music part of their civilization before that civilization was destroyed. It was a civilization of peace and love; a kinship with all life forms of the natural earth.

You too can tap into the ancient skills of your spiritual ancestors and use music to heal your social brain. Many young people who could not afford psychotherapy used Hip Hop music as a way of owning their traumatic history. Music impacts all areas of the brain. To move out of the negativity bias of the brain, you can reprogram the brain using music. You might do this by repeating positive words of affirmation with a beat and rhythm. Find songs with words and rhythms that encapsulate positive thoughts and self-healing. Dance and sing with these rhythms.

Or use sign-language with the words of the music. I once started a sign-language choir at a mental health clinic with patients who had diagnoses of schizophrenia, bipolar, anxiety, and depression. All were on medication. Our sign language music was about love and peace. Patients who had profound fears and rageful thoughts were able to transcend their thinking. They did so well that they were able to perform at a beautiful resort in New Rochelle, New York. Their performance brought tears to everyone's eyes. Many of Michael Jackson's songs are healing, such as "We Are the World," which is a message of hope. His music can also make you want to get up and move your body.

The music of Lionel Richie; Earth, Wind & Fire; Luther Vandross; Johnny Mathis; and Roberta Flack lets you know that pain is real, but you can transcend it with love and trade it for joy and happiness. I find jazz to be most healing. I like artists like jazz violinist Jean Luc Ponty, jazz pianist Bob James, and music like "A Day in a Life," by Wes Montgomery is just so beautiful and healing for me when I feel overwhelmed with negative thoughts. Music can engage your brain in such a way that it improves cognitive functioning, pleasurable sensations, movement, stress reduction, and your health

(Sternberg, 2013). And you get to experience the beauty of our world accompanied by rhythms and words of affirmation.

4. Do not fight or do things that will cause a fight (angry hormones)

I know this may be difficult for some people, but practice this for 30 days. Society teaches us to solve conflict with fist, gun, angry retaliation, and even wars. Remember, you are reprogramming your brain so that the neural connections allow you to touch the world with loving kindness, and not maul it with killer rage or hostile anger. There will always be conflict and pain in our world, but you don't have to fight. What you do need are protective concern and the skills to assert yourself.

My son took karate classes when he was young so that he would learn the skills of respect, honoring others, and, at times, protecting himself. He grew up with the concept of saying No to fighting, but knowing that we live in a world where one may need self-defense. The only thing fighting does is assault your brain with tons of cortisol hormones that will negatively affect you mentally and physically. The more you build up those angry hormones, the more your brain is prone to fighting. By the time my son was twelve years old, he no longer had ADHD. Many children with ADHD have fight/flight reactions, and fight/flight can become an addiction.

I had a client who had been born while her mother was in prison, and she didn't know her dad. She was an attractive lady, and she was in a relationship when she came to see me. When she got angry, she could be physical with her partner. Her partner had been in prison and did not want to return, but he was at his wits' end as to how to relate to my client, who would yell, scream, and hit. My female client had been programmed to fight back, not to be taken advantage of, and to say whatever was on her mind, which was mainly negative, and judgmental.

By the time she was in her thirties, she had cancer. She was consumed with angry hormones and had depleted her healthy hormones because of the brain and body connection. Because of negative thoughts, she was not fit. She could not remember her mother ever smiling at her or saying words like, "*I love you.*" The idea of waking up and making positive statements about herself or thinking of what she could be grateful for was foreign to her.

In her social brain healing exercise, she developed awareness of her social brain, as an angry brain, which impacts relationships. She completed the following:

	EVENTS CAUSING EMOTIONAL INJURY	EMOTIONS IMPACTING YOUR BRAIN
CHILDHOOD	Parents did not create a family for me. Their needs came first. I was born in prison. Mom drug-addicted/in prison. Dad in prison, maybe for life.	SHAME, FEAR, ANGER, RESENTMENT DISAPPOINTMENT
ADOLESCENCE	Judgments by peers because I did not have the best clothes; I was in foster care. Attracted to bad-boy types. Having a child before financial independence	POOR SELF-ESTEEM
ADULT	Enemy-memories Blaming others Victim mentality	REVENGE, RAGE

Her first step was to own what had happened to her that had contributed to rage and anger. By doing so, she owned up to the fact that there was neural brain channels for rage and anger.

The second step was the Serenity Prayer, the process of tapping into the divine higher power of your wise mind to strengthen the PFC (prefrontal cortex) pathway and to create a state of serenity, humbleness, and loving kindness by stating, *"Grant me the serenity to accept the things I cannot change:"* my parents, boss, boyfriend or the past. She learned that when she was fighting, she was trying to change someone or was punishing someone. She had to let go of trying to change other people.

The third step was being mindful that fighting was an addiction for her, just like a drug addiction. We would take it one day at a time, but she had to commit to saying No to fighting, to smile, and to use the DNA extraction techniques: no to fighting, no to profanity, no to clutter, yes to exercise, yes to healthy diet, etc. because that was something she had the power to do; she could change herself. She had power over her own emotional responses. After a couple of weeks, she could feel the difference when she was calm, smiling, and not fighting. She was starting to reprogram her brain and defrost the HPA. Remember we are all connected as a human family, your actions of fighting and being hateful has a trickle down dynamic impacting and affecting the entire planet.

5. Exercise for happy hormones

The happy hormone endorphin is released after just a few minutes of exercise, such as dancing for fifteen minutes. When you exercise, you are saying that you care about you. You should smile while you exercise: it's a positive affirmation. The world may be putting you down, your mother may not smile at you, your boss may not recognize all the effort you are exerting on the job, or your spouse may make critical statements, but you can stimulate your happy hormones and say *I care about me.* If your BMI (body mass index)

is in the obesity range, you may be self-medicating with food. Please note that not every obese person is self-medicating with food; some people eat very little and are obese due to medical factors.

Start every morning with generating your happy hormones say your five positive affirmations, smile and be grateful; and do fifteen minutes of exercise. Get some sleep, try to get up early, and eat right, not compulsively—you deserve those happy hormones.

6. Start a calming journal to heal the neurobiology of the Angry Brain

Don't try to avoid confrontation. Sometimes you must take a stand for your position or you will suffer from unresolved anger and frustration. Denial and being withdrawn or sulking will not increase your happy hormones. Rather than bottling up frustration, start a calming journal to heal the neurobiology of the angry brain. The neurobiology of the angry brain refers to retaliation and rage, which as you know by now, leads to poor mental and physical health. Write down what you are angry or frustrated about. You may suffer from unresolved anger that has accumulated over your lifespan. Know what you are angry about, get in touch with repressed memories or enemy memories, seek professional help but learn to delete neural pathways contaminated with rage. Most days you should be saying or writing in your journal *"I am happy, I'm okay."*

Do a genogram or a family history tree. What is your ancestral karma? What happened in the history of your ancestors that impact you today? What ancestral karma contributes to your rage that impacts you today? I have had clients who killed their love ones such as a parent, spouse or a friend. When asked why, the common reply is drugs, they snapped because of the rage, or the devil. My assessment is ancestral karma in some cases. In the case of Mrs. Johnson, the woman in chapter 6, I feared for her young children. One day the dynamics of her ancestral karma related to being Black was going to impact them; in fact it was already having an impact. Get it out on paper. Did your parents curse, yell, abuse, or abandon you? What was their ancestral karma? Go back in history to fully understand ancestral karma and delete those things you have no control over.

Use or develop your PFC (prefrontal cortex) or the wise mind to heal the angry brain and overcome pain and suffering. Avoid using your emotional mind, which can lead to the excessive use of alcohol, drugs, or food. Write down coping strategies. You can list ways to wisely handle your situation thus, using your wise mind, which is not id-centered. It is not your emotional or rational mind. Your rational mind will tell you that you have a right to be angry and rageful. Your rational mind will tell you that you have a right to get drunk and wild-out. Yes you do have a right to be angry when bad things happen to you; but the reality of the world is that bad things happen. You can choose to be the spiritual warrior for love and kindness not for hate, retaliation or revenge.

My client Mrs. Scott learned how to use her calming journal to prepare her for conversations with her husband. She would write over and over "I'm okay." When I first met Mrs. Scott, she suffered many medical problems, had just had a surgery, although a young lady in her early thirties. She was in a relationship with an older man who had 4 children and was also dealing with his ex-wife. Mrs. Scott became infuriated whenever the ex-wife was involved. She and her husband were yelling at each other, he was drinking excessively, and she at times was physically aggressive towards him. She felt that these arguments were making her physically ill, and she had gained over 100 pounds.

Mrs. Scott ancestral karma led her to choose a partner where she could express her repressed angry brain. As a child she had been obedient and never a problem for her parents, teachers or siblings. She was always the responsible person helping everyone. Now she was in a relationship where she was being overly helpful, but feeling she was not getting the love she deserved. Subsequently, she was having major temper tantrums in her relationship. Her first assignment for healing the neurobiology of her angry brain was to say *"no to fighting"* for 30 days and to write in her calming journal. She could not argue loudly or aggressively with anyone for 30 days.

Over the first thirty days, she completed her family tree. She committed to not arguing back or reacting to her husband with a temper tantrum, and agreed to the tips for increasing happy hormones. Before starting this exercise, she sat down and calmly told her husband that at times she feels physically ill when they argue. She said *"she loved him and felt he was a great father."* Mrs. Scott agreed to write all her angry words, even profanity in her calming journal, but could not use these words with her husband or others. She could also use her journal to plan something positive like a date night for her and husband. While her husband was yelling or arguing, she practiced and took deep breaths in and out and quietly listened to the core message he was trying to convey, or at times she went to her room and sat quietly. Over the first thirty-day period that she was able to adhere to the plan, her stress level decreased; over sixty days of adherence, she stopped having panic attacks and was able to smile. Since she was not arguing with her husband, he would say, *"The therapy is helping you,"* and she would just smile and say thank you. Over time, she and her husband developed an improved way of communicating, and her husband became active in AA (Alcohol Anonymous meetings). Mrs. Scott continued to use her calming journal to help with coping strategies and to acknowledge upset and angry feelings.

7. Find Love and increase your oxytocin and endorphins (happy hormones)

Finding something you love to do or, better yet, finding someone to love is another way to stimulate your happy hormones and a neurochemistry wire for loving others. In the beginning of our work together, John had no real concept of loving anything. The neurochemicals that would allow a person to trust and show loving kindness was very weak. The good thing is that the brain is receptive to new information and can create circuits and wiring for a new physical foundation. John decided he would love to work. It was decided that he would do a service for others, so he worked in the hospital deli. He smiled and did not argue with the customers. He was caring. He was so happy when he was able to earn enough to buy gifts and show love to two of his younger siblings. Cultivate your love relationships, by saying words like *I love you*. Giving someone a hug or smile can spread happiness to others.

8. Don't take things personally

Dr. Hanson, a neuropsychologist who is an invited speaker at Oxford, Harvard, and Stanford Universities says, *"Don't take things personally"* (Hanson, 2011). John often had temper tantrums in the class room: knocking over desks, yelling, screaming, and cursing so that a Code Red would be called and numerous people would show up to restrain him. When asked what made him go off, it was always that someone said or did something to him that he did not like.

"Okay, John, what happened today?"

"Mitchell called me dumb and said I can't read."

"Okay, John, do you have problems reading?

"Yes, I do."

John was impulsive, had a frozen HPA, a hyperarousal state, and poor prefrontal cortex pathway function which was needed to slow his emotional mind when it was triggered. John practiced not taking things personally and not being id-centered as part of developing skills for narcissistic resistance. Being id-centered means that everything is about you, and when you don't get your way you have a temper tantrum or become depressed and withdrawn.

The father of psychology, Dr. Freud described three parts of the psyche that impact our interactions with others and our mental health: they are the Id, the Ego, and the Superego. The Id contains our uncontrolled drives and impulses. The Superego seeks to control the id, like a good policeman or policewoman who stops the crime and the violence. The Ego serves as a mediator between the id and the policewoman. John had little superego development to tell him to stop doing something because it is not the right thing to do. But once he was given the right tools for progressive mental health and happiness, he was a fast learner. He became less id-centered and more spiritually centered. Being spiritually centered means you think of others not just yourself. Being spiritually centered means you are open to listening to the criticisms of others without suffering. John learned that he could actually make positive spiritual contributions to his community by being able to accept that he can't always have things his way and there are times that he may make mistakes as no one is perfect.

The more you can *accept* not getting your way, the happier you will be. The more you can *accept* the reality of differences and there will be conflicts, the stronger your PFC pathway. The more you can *accept*, the more you will be able to think of others. The more you *do not accept* and take things personally, the more unhappy and miserable you will be, decreasing those neurochemicals you need for happiness and positive mental health. You may end up living in a hospital or prison, be easily fired, or be addicted to drugs, alcohol, or food. John chose *not* to be id-centered. He learned not to take things personally, and after that, he never had another temper tantrum.

9. Do the right thing: Strengthen your prefrontal cortex (PFC). Don't be Stereotyped

Be your natural self. You don't have to behave like the dysfunctional people you see on TV. They act dysfunctional as a form of entertainment and may be earning millions of dollars. We know that the brain has a negativity bias so we do like watching negative actions. Unless you are getting million dollars to be dysfunctional, to use profanity, or to be a fighter, like Mike Tyson—be your natural self, and go with the natural positive flow of things. Fighting with your spouse will not earn you a million dollars. Abstain from cursing, lying, stealing, and being critical. You don't have to agree with others, but you do not have to fight about it or be dysfunctional. You may have a temperament that is irritable and negative you will have to work harder to stimulate the happy hormones.

Have the right actions. For example, if you speak English, then speak it correctly. Be your natural self. Correctly speaking a language does not mean you are not being your natural self, it just shows that you have a developed PFC. Did you watch the movie *The Pursuit of Happiness* with Will Smith? Watch it to get a clearer understanding of doing the right things to strengthen your PFC. Doing the right thing, using the right speech, and acting right will move the neural connections of your brain towards a positive and healthy lifestyle. At the same time, you do not deplete your healthy neurochemicals, like serotonin.

By doing the right thing, you improve your PFC, the part of the brain that helps you slow down your reactive fight/flight responses. John is a good example. He could not read and he was highly reactive, so his PFC development had not started. He could not sit in a classroom for more than a few minutes. Once he started social brain healing, his new actions stimulated the happy hormones and healthy brain neural activity, and he moved away from actions that depleted healthy neural chemicals such as dopamine and serotonin. Subsequently, his learning ability drastically improved. He was able to sit in the class for the entire time required, and his teachers found him a joy to work with.

10. Have High Aspirations-Avoid Being Stereotyped: (having goals increases dopamine)

The social illness of narcissism is real; it is an intrinsic part of life. In a competitive world, those with overt narcissism hurt others, and find ways and strategies to maintain superiority, power, and control. Subsequently, many of you suffer from covert narcissism, or trauma-linked narcissism, which is the type of narcissism John had. Trauma-linked narcissism can respond to psychotherapy and social brain healing.

Some people have a combination overt and covert narcissism that will be difficult to treat (Kernberg, 2007). John just had covert narcissism. If you suffer from trauma-linked narcissism, you can heal yourself with the elements of social brain healing. Start with saying positive affirmations, cultivating high aspirations and a purpose for your life, say No to fighting, and remember you are a human, a member of the human family and not a stereotype. If you are a student—and it doesn't matter whether you are fifteen, forty, or eighty, go to school and be the best student you can be. Don't think I'm too old or I'm this or that, just study hard: do all your assignments and never be late to class unless it is a real emergency.

In 1996, I went to a college for computer programming. At the time, I did not even know how to turn on a computer. Most of the students were much younger and had already taken computer courses. At the time, I did not know how to type. At my job, I had a secretary; I recorded my reports using a tape recorder, and she typed them for me. I had developed the *do-the-right-thing attitude* and high aspirations along with teaching my son, and I used those positive neural brain pathways in my computer programming courses. I did *not* think, *"Oh, I can't do this because I don't even know how to turn on a computer, so I will never learn how to program one."* I thought instead *the brain is not hard-wire and I can learn just like my much younger co-students.* With positive goals, I subsequently graduated summa cum laude in courses that were significantly challenging. Many of my instructors did not believe I had no prior training in computers. I had graduated from college with a BS degree in psychology in 1973 and a MS degree in clinical social work in 1975, way before computer classes were commonplace.

When you go to school, you may encounter a teacher with overt narcissism or xenophobia who tries to break your high aspirations, especially if you are talented and bright and have lots of new ideas. Don't fight; don't develop a negative attitude; just do what you can and learn all that you can. One day, I hope, we will have lawyers who practice educational malpractice. An American who gets a 98 or 95 on a Regents exam or a high score on a SAT exam should not end up with a class grade of 65. This actually happened to someone I knew when he was in high school.

The reality of our culture is that it is competitive, and it could be that not all professors or teachers want to help talented Americans of African descent achieve PhDs or get into top universities like Harvard or Columbia. Currently, there are not many legal or inexpensive methods to fight this competitive strategy. I refer to it as *educational malpractice*. Our society is more motivated to take legal actions related to crimes and violence. Without educational malpractice, we don't have a vehicle for fighting back against a school or university system, thus many students do get pushed out.

Nonetheless, that is no reason to give up on high aspirations. My friend, who was a brilliant person, with the high score on his SAT exam, could not get into the better colleges because of his low grades, but he did get into the finance corps in the army. Yes, you will feel pain and disappointment when your hard work is blocked. But remember, you live in a world where pain is inevitable and xenophobia exists, and that is overt narcissism. You cannot fight back with rage every time someone hurts you or you will retard the neurochemicals in your brain, freeze your HPA, and damage your greatest asset—your brain.

What you can do to meet your high aspirations and move toward progressive happiness is....

- If you are a worker, go to work, smile, be cordial, say hello to co-workers, and do the best job you can do. Do not complain. *Oh, this job! This person is rude, the boss is a pain in my....*" It is not the right attitude for success, for meeting high aspirations on the job, or for your brain health. Remember complaining behavior depletes the healthy hormones in your brain, stimulates victim mentality, and leads to physical illness. A good thing about the world you live in is that there are unions; if you are not receiving your rightful pay or treatment, you can talk to someone. If you are being discriminated against, there are laws to protect you. Sometimes they work, but sometimes they don't. Sometimes lawyers help and sometimes they do not—a reality of the world we currently live in.

Remember, if you have ideas, learn and start your own business.

11. Knowledge is power and a way to end victim mentality

To have the power of knowledge, you must first see and acknowledge the beauty around you and the advances of the human race. In our world there is much to enjoy, much to motivate us, despite the fact that others' competitiveness, xenophobia, and narcissism may seek to undermine your goals, your talents, and your life purpose. Nonetheless, withstand, withstand, and withstand it. Move forward with your high aspirations, keeping the light of knowledge burning brilliantly in your social brain. Be inventive and add to all the beauty of the planet that already exists.

With knowledge as power, you are aware of the good and the bad. You can make the choice to contribute towards the good. You can also own your painful experiences. Write on the picture of the brain in Chapter 10, draw a brain in your calming journal. Say, *"Yes, this painful experience did happen, but I'm moving forward."* When Hiroshima was blown up during World War II, the Japanese acknowledged that yes, we fought a war, we lost—now what can we do to rebuild our country? They used their ability to acquire knowledge and were able to recreate and rebuild. The Japanese, who came here to America, did not allow xenophobia or the strategies of hurtful and hateful competition to impede their ability to acquire knowledge and later to contribute to their ethnic birthplace. They used family as a tool and coping strategy for their success in the present and for future success of their descendants.

If you had trauma as a child, adolescent, or adult, use the concept of knowledge is power to create forward thinking of not being a victim. Mrs. Aceveda was a client of mine. In her seventies, she was a highly religious lady and a grandmother. When I started seeing Mrs. Aceveda, she had been prosecuted for a crime; a felony. She denied that she had ever been involved in any criminal activities.

She reported that she had financially helped a neighbor, who had used her help in a criminal manner and without her knowledge. The neighbor had reported that she was involved. Mrs. Aceveda could not understand how she could have been charged with a felony, and now she would have to go to trial.

In my work with her, she gained the knowledge that bad things can happen to good people. I asked her to tell me the story of Jesus Christ. He was a good man, yet he was crucified on the cross. Knowledge shows us that we all have crosses to bear, but you can use knowledge to keep you from getting stuck in victim mentality. When Mrs. Aceveda was found guilty in court, she had sufficient power of knowledge from our sessions together to accept her cross. She also took her legal steps for an appeal. Fortunately, she was given house arrest and was not placed in prison. To show her gratitude for her improved state of mind, she continued to do missionary work for others, as a community service.

Mrs. Aceveda was able to reprogram her brain for happiness and progressive mental health. She was able spread happiness to others, increase her happy hormones, and her mental health remained intact. When bad things happen, you are at risk of being traumatized, feeling hopeless, which negatively impacts brain chemistry. Mrs. Aceveda started using affirmations, meditation, and having the knowledge to know that no one is beyond bearing the weight of the cross. Bad things happen to good people is a reality of the world. These practices helped her to transcend victim mentality.

12. Learn Sign Language: The language of peace

In 2014, I traveled to Istanbul, Turkey—such a beautiful country. While there, I was at a bus depot, eating in a small café, when three men entered and sat at a table near me. I do not speak the Turkish language except for a few words, but when I saw that these three men were deaf and signing, I felt such joy. I communicated with them for a short while; they were equally happy to be able to talk to an American when others could not. When I boarded the bus, we said *"love and peace"* to each other. Sitting on the bus, I thought how wonderful it would be if all members of the human family would learn Sign Language. I felt a kinship with the Turkish men, and they with me, simply because we were able to communicate in Sign Language.

I think of sign language as the language of peace and it has a calming element. Rather than yelling and cursing at your children when you are upset, practice using some signs for *stop, please, time-out*. Using signs without the extremes of body language keeps you calmer than words, from my experience. There are no evidence-based trials for this, but I have used signs with younger clients who paid closer attention and smiled when verbal words were not used. Many children and adolescents are traumatized by yelling. Using sign language also made it easier to assess trauma experiences in young and even adolescent clients. If signing can help you stay calmer, then you are keeping your brain chemistry regulated towards calmness. Additionally, learning a new language improves your PFC pathway (Katz & Rubin, 1999).

When I conducted the sign-language choir with hearing adults who attended a mental health clinic during the day, one woman in the group suffered from severe panic attacks and at times feared leaving her home. While in the sign language group, she never missed a group meeting. All the clients were highly motivated to attend and happy that they did not have to talk since the music did it for them. We had plans to perform at an event at the Devonport Country Club in New Rochelle. None of the clients in the group had ever preformed in front of an audience. The woman with the severe panic attacks said she would not be able to attend or perform. However, with daily practice, the clients grew more self-satisfied. She had learned a new language that improved her PFC pathway and slowed down her emotional reactions, and she looked forward to coming to the sign-language choir therapy groups. Subsequently, this client with the severe panic attacks performed at the fund raising event in front of many people. This woman with the panic attacks did not have even a small attack of anxiety, and she felt so happy.

13. Be forgiving

Everyone makes mistakes. Besides making mistakes, people do bad and even evil things; it's unfortunate when those bad things become a part of *your* world. *Grant me the serenity to accept the things I cannot change*—other people and the past. What you *can* change is you. You can be a positive, spiritual individual who contributes to world peace and with loving kindness towards others. Forgiveness is the only way to heal your brain and body from the horrific actions of others. Jesus Christ taught us about forgiveness when he was being crucified on the cross. He said *"God forgive them for they know not what they do."* Of course, people do know when they are doing bad things for their own self-interest. What they do *not* know is how their bad and evil behavior destroys the emotional and mental health fiber of the entire world. Imagine that one act of hate and violence has the impact of an exploding volcano on the mental health of the entire human race, and this they do *not* know, but now you know.

Just recently, on June 17, 2015, a man with overt narcissism walked into a church during bible study time in Charleston, North Carolina, and killed nine people at a historically African American church. His self-interest was to divide the races. Why divide the races with hate? We all share a common ancestry, the humanoid ancestry. His behavior was a trigger for an African American's retaliation. An

African American, who had suffered from being discriminated and carried around in his brain unresolved rage deposits. This African American reporter gunned down European American reporters, whom he knew, claiming they were racist and that he was triggered by the Charleston shootings. This situation in Charleston is an illustration of overt narcissism that continues to exist in our world.. It is not much different from the lynching of Arthur Steven in 1933. The African American reaction is covert narcissism. We have not as a human race done the emotional evolving needed to stop the tornados of hate or bombs of retaliation, so the tornados, bombs and volcanos keep exploding and polluting our mental health. We all must be strong, learn to deal constructively with anger, and not allow actions that we have no control over to dictate who we are, where we are going or to undermine our mental health and create thoughts of killer rage.

Your brain is your greatest asset. You can program it so that the behaviors of others' now or the past are just one of the realities of the world you live in. Yes, it happened, but you have the power and courage to withstand the impact of the punch and move forward. Once you turn off the DNA channels that make you want to retaliate with aggression and killer rage, you will see the beauty of your greatest asset—your social brain. Do not allow the behaviors of others to chronically release anger hormones into your mind and body and influence your wellness and your happiness.

We all experience anger, but your anger should not lead to rage and retaliation that hurts others. Some might say to me, *"If I had that experience with the professors, I would have gone to the Dean's home and burnt it down."* There are people who resort to arson when angry. Acts of aggressive retaliation pollutes the planet for Karma of destruction. In my opinion, it is behaviors such as the KKK, their hate and aggression, which indirectly led to the destruction of the twin towers in New York City, decades or centuries later. Just imagine what our world would be like today, if members of the KKK had loved and been supportive of their neighbors who were different and millions of others supported their leadership of love and support. Take a few minutes to reflect on your world and what it would be like today had leadership been rooted in love and support.

Today in the world we are the only humans who survived. There were other humans that are today extinct like the Neanderthals. Maybe, my theory, they became extinct because of violence. Today, we as modern humans are busy building weapons to kill each other, rather than learning how to live in peace. You as a reader of this book can learn to live with peace and forgiveness for events that you have no control over:

I live in a beautiful world where pain is inevitable, where toxic people kill others for self-interest. Even if you are kind and good, you can be hurt, killed, or abused for no reason. I will commit to be the spiritual force who brings about progressive mental health and progressive peace and happiness to my world and to all my neighbors. I feel the pain and anger of this event, (_____), but I make the choice not to suffer or give in to killer rage because of this painful event. I must <u>accept</u> the reality of my world, <u>accept</u> that in it are hate, envy, abuse, and evil. I will transcend this component of the world I live in with forgiveness and do what is positive and spiritually right. I let go of my pain for my own wellness, and I choose to release (_____) from my prosecution, from my punishment, and from my killer rage due to his/her wrongdoings, *which may have or had lawful consequences. I choose to move forward. I will make use of my wise mind and have the courage to change myself for the sake of a better world, better relationships, and more loving kindness on the planet.*

14. Our Ancestors, The First Humans and The Kinship with all life forms

The happy hormones are something we inherited from the first humans the Africans. PFC knowledge requires knowing your ethnic heritage, the first humans of Africa. PFC knowledge is not emotional knowledge; it is an executive function. It is important to have some knowledge of how humans evolved. How the human brain evolved for love and attachment with others. I suggested that you watch the PBS show or buy the CD on the first humans of Africa. How did behaviors of hate, violence and subsequent retaliation begin? We can answer this question with PFC knowledge not emotional knowledge.

The history of human love and attachment ranges from the evolution of the first modern humans, the Africans. There were other humans, who came much later, such as the Neanderthal humans, but they are extinct. The Neanderthals of Europe may have spent thousands of years in freezing climates and/or with a scarceness of food. These impoverished conditions may have intensified competition in aggressive ways for resources. The first African humans had a civilization of peace and a kinship with all life forms. Centuries later we had the imperialists. We had wars, murders, oppression, and hateful genocide. Human aggression against others as we know it today has historical, biological, and cultural elements. We have learned that some individuals have an inborn nature or temperament to attack or hate others (Kagan, 2010). We also know of the brain's neuroplasticity, thus individuals can change if they are willing to feed and strengthen that pathway of the brain for love of others.

Today, world history is based on the written words of the more aggressive and violent civilizations. It is a fact of life that many of the more spiritual, non-aggressive civilizations were a part of prehistory. Many written materials about the first modern humans of Africa have been eradicated from what is currently known as the historical period (Jackson, 1970). The peaceful and spiritual civilizations were destroyed by the patriarchal, overtly narcissistic civilizations characterization of emotional health by aggression, violence, domination, and exerting control over others through violence and enslavement.

The civilization of the first humans was a civilization of hard workers. The first modern humans originated in Africa and travelled though out the world. Based on DNA results these African first humans the homo sapiens travelled to Europe, Asia, and interbred with archaic humans the Neanderthals who occupied Europe and Asia creating hybrid offspring. Many non-African people today carry a small percentage of Neanderthal DNA; or Denisovans DNA another archaic human primarily from Asia. See: http://www.pbs.org/first-peoples/episodes/africa/.

Neanderthals are extinct today perhaps because their harsh lifestyles and competition for resources led to aggression and violence. The first humans of Africa survived because of their ability for a non-violent kinship with all life forms (Diop, 1974). That ability referred to as totemism allowed the brains of the first modern humans to acquire the circuitry, the neurochemistry, and neurotransmitters which generated and maintained positive thoughts, trusting, and happy attachments to others. Subsequently, the neurochemistry of the first modern humans related to kinship with others or love of our neighbors exist today in our DNA.

Africans, the first modern humans had written languages, amassed libraries, and were pioneers in the sciences, architecture, medicine, and a peaceful way of life—and all of it was totally eradicated from world history. However, there are currently many archeologist and geneticist of European descent who seek the truth of how humans evolved, like Dr. Spencer Wells, see Journey of man: a Genetic Odyssey. Of course there will be those who will continue to destroy or camouflaging the history of the first modern human. Nonetheless, the civilization of the first humans was stolen. We can refer to the location in Africa as Ta-Meri or Ta-Merry. More aggressive civilizations copied, plagiarized, altered, destroyed, and changed the name to Egypt (see Diop, 1974; James, 1954; Williams, 1987 and ben-Jochannan, 1989). The first humans had a matriarchal social system in which women were free and life was spiritually oriented. This matriarchal social system was eradicated due to the rise of the aggressive and violent patriarchal social system (Diop, 1974). Although, this aggressive social system made vast contributions, we honor this aggressive violent civilization without pointing out the weaknesses related to connecting as a peaceful human family.

Millions, of years ago, early species evolved from mutations of protozoan to wormlike animals to crustaceans and insects. Later, a new group of animals, the chordate, evolved. The branch of fish gave rise to amphibians, reptiles, birds, and mammals that nourished their offspring with milk. From egg-laying species evolved the pouched animals that proliferated into the monkeys and apes. Hairy apes evolved into less hairy humans (La Barre, 1954). Less hairy humans became what is now known as the first homo sapiens, the humanoids, the Africans. The evolution of the species or humans can be determined by mutations overtime and by mitochondrial DNA comprised of chromosomes and genes, which is inherited by the female—mitochondrial Eve. Compared to primates, hairlessness traits are humanoid traits. Monkeys and apes have straight hair and thin lips, where the more humanoid trait was kinky hair and thick lips are the traits of the first modern humans the homo-sapiens. The animal trait was body hairiness whereas the humanoid trait was body hairlessness (La Barre, 1954). Later, we have the archaic human; these were the hairy humans, the Neanderthals. To learn more about what is written here about the first humans and hybrid humans see:

http://www.pbs.org/first-peoples/episodes/africa/; And, see http://www.pbs.org/first-peoples/episodes/australia/.

Social evolution of the ancient Homo sapiens civilization in East Africa was based on matriarchal leadership. This system of matriarchal leadership was referred to by anthropologist as "Mother's Right" (Jackson, 1970). During this period existed the civilized idea of respect for animals and plants, which was referred to as *totemism*. Totemism recognized that God or a divine spirit loves variety; thus, other animals and plants were viewed as kinfolk deserving of mutual rights. The first modern humans were not xenophobic. This may also have made it easy for the African first human to breed with the archaic Neanderthals, and produce the hybrid human, which we have today.

The first ancient civilizations worshipped heavenly bodies and followed totemic practices signifying divine kinship amongst different species or different groups. The contribution of a civilization that honored mother's rights and considered dedicated to a peaceful and spiritual coexistence with all of life has been destroyed. In the totemic first human ancient world, a boy held the highest respect for all men in his community or tribe, the belief being that any man in his tribe could have been his father (Jackson, 1970). The same respect was applied to women, the belief being that any woman in the tribe could have been her mother. This sense of kinship within groups of people may have grown out of an advanced social mental health, wherein the infantile needs of the self-centered transcended to the spiritual needs of the community for survival, happiness, social peace, and harmony despite differences.

The first humans, the Africans were also a civilization in which the biological temperament of the people was peaceful and accepting of differences (Diop, 1974). This civilization was ultimately destroyed, but the first humans have lived on and their DNA is shared with the new group of humans coming thousands of years later, the hybrid human, today all humans share African genes/ancestry.

With the advancement of the hybrids, the civilization of kinship, brotherhood and sisterhood with all life forms became extinct as men became Gods due to their physical strength, acquired property, weapons, and ability to own people as property or to kill them as entertainment. The newer civilizations, had roots in what we know theoretically today is related to aggression, narcissism, and the role of instincts. Such theories of human violence were explained by Sigmund Freud in his paper. "Instincts and Their Vicissitudes."

Instincts are developed within the biological dynamic of the organism. Internal excitation is constant and only terminates when the instinctual need has been fulfilled. The instinctual process is based on the nervous system's attempts to contend with an intrinsic effort of self-satisfaction for food and sex (Eros). For Freud, the concept of instinct had both psychological and biological determinants (Monte, 1980). Freud also proposed that humans have a death wish (thanatos). Thanatos, the death wish, is the opposite of Eros, which aims to embrace all that life has to offer. An infant or child who is deprived of food is strongly impelled to aggressively seek food, yelling, screaming, and kicking for self-satisfaction. Or the child may have the temperament to use self-satisfaction methods such as thumb-sucking for peaceful complacency. The temperament of thumb-sucking allows for self-satisfaction and concerns for others. Or the child gives up and turns to the death wish, leading to behaviors of self-destruction.

Another theory was proposed by Konrad Lorenz, a Nobel Peace Prize scientist who claimed that human aggression is shared with animal aggression, perhaps the instincts of the Neanderthals, the "fighting instinct" for survival of the fittest by means of violence and control. Over the course of evolution, this fighting instinct ensured that "the strongest individuals will pass their genes to the next generation" (Baron & Byrne, 2003, p. 436). "The strongest" means the one with the ability to kill and destroy another. This survival-of-the-fittest civilization, which was rooted in the instinct to fight, is the civilization that dominates our brain energies today. With the rise of industrialization and the theory of survival of the fittest, we lost the teachings of the earlier, non-aggressive civilization, our first ancestors.

Many of the first African humans in historic times spent centuries trying to escape the destruction of the fighting-instinct humans that invaded East Africa, which led to raping the women and stealing their land, their language, their writings, and their medical skills (Diop, 1974). Those of the first humans who were most determined escaped and traveled for centuries throughout all parts of Africa and beyond. The long periods of wandering all over the continent of Africa, often aimlessly, comprised the great historic race for survival of the first humans.

This migration of a once-great ancient people, who had thousands of years ago traveled the world, was now splintered into countless independent societies and chiefdoms, all with different dialects (Diop, 1974). Some Africans were able to override the adversities of migration and created highly developed societies. Because of the suffering involved in escaping and traveling in unknown areas, followed later by centuries of forced enslavement in America, many of the first African humans suffered and many lost the ability for self-actualization and inventiveness that their ancient pre-historic ancestors had. In the next and final chapter, you will learn the thumb-sucking skills of our spiritual ancestors who did not lose the ability of self-actualization and inventiveness. They epitomized the quest for kinship with all life forms contributing to a peaceful civilization.

CHAPTER 10

STRATEGIES FROM OUR SPIRITUAL ANCESTORS FOR PROGRESSIVE MENTAL HEALTH, HAPPINESS & AN END TO RAGE

On July of 1988, I walked out of the courtroom after my case against Schering Plough and Mt. Sinai Hospital. There had not been one African American on the jury, only Whites. One woman on the jury came out with a smile on her face. I was stunned by their decision of no compensation for my son's disabilities when the medication given to me intravenously was known to cause birth defects in animals. As I left the courthouse in New York City, I could barely walk. I sat on a bench for a few hours. During that time, memories of my great-grandfather, Promise Mayfield, came to my mind. My great-grandfather had been born a slave and suffered all the pains of the world back in the 1800s with slavery and Jim Crow. I realized that the all-White courtroom I had just left had a cultural nature to hating others who are different nothing had really changed; the pharmaceutical lawyer had said to the all-White jury, we have to test drugs on someone. My Great Grandfather would tell me I did the best I could to fight for my son's right to compensation. He believed that no matter what your situation, every day that you are alive you have the opportunity to make the world a better place, and hoarding rage would not make the world a better place nor will I grow as a spiritual human. That day in July of 1988, I had to learn to thumb-suck.

THE THUMB-SUCKING THEORY AND EMOTIONAL INTELLIGENCE OF THE
HUMAN SPIRIT

This belief that you can make the world a better place is the premise
of the thumb-sucking theory. From science we have learned that
energy cannot be created or destroyed it can only be changed. We
currently live in a world where the energy is focused on negativity;
so bad things can happen. However, there are unified energy fields
for peace and calmness like the infant that chooses thumb-sucking
over yelling. However, yelling, screaming and kicking are normal
behaviors for the infant. But where does this thumb-sucking energy
come from?

This energy for coping with the harsh elements of life has roots
to the first humans who were highly sociable humanoids. They
originated from a collective community that believed in a kinship
with all life forms, unlike the separate family units that we have
today. The first African humans had an emotional intelligence of
peace and calmness that allowed them the ability to travel the earth.
They were able to thumb suck, accept the realities of life, create,
love, laugh, dance, sing, and interbred with those who were different.
This all translates to the fact that we the descendants have inherited
neural pathways for empathy for others and self-love for expanding
our horizons. All thanks to the first modern humans who survived
the harshness of life, so that we are all here today. Was their survival
for us to hate and kill each other or to love and honor?

When you think of DNA, imagine neural pathways as having
various routes. Route A, route D, route L, route S and route W; thus,
pathways ADLSW. Imagine we all have all the biologically pathways:
A_D_L_S_W. Currently route D for dysfunctional behaviors may
be a strong neural pathway. Route L for love and kindness may be

weak. We have the biological ability to strengthen route L; to have a kinship with all our fellow humans as brothers, sisters, or cousins referred to as the ta-merrian way or simply learning how to thumb-suck for peace.

My great grandfather, despite his suffering, became a minister. He had a strong pathway for route W, working hard. He believed in spiritual capitalism, meaning that indigenous to capitalism was the helping hand component. If you open a store to start a business for your own success, you also provide jobs for your employees, and you can be kind to those employees who work hard to make your business a success. This allows your employees to earn an income and to buy things for their children, their spouse, or for themselves. You can do things to make others happy, and help those who work for your company to prosper.

Spiritual capitalism allows and encourages competition, but fair competition, ethical behavior, and acceptance of the contributions of others without envy. My great grandfather encouraged those who attended his church to save and own property, even a small piece of land. He took up collections to help those in need, like members of his church who owned property, but had problems with the finances. Nonetheless, his ministry led to him being placed in prison for his preaching to the members of his church the value of economics and owning property or land. He had the strong belief that God helps those who help themselves. I believe he had the energy and the brain neural synapses of the first modern humans; for he was a peaceful survivor. When he came out of prison, he said to those in his church, "Let's pray." It was the energetic force of my great-grandfather within me that made it possible for me to stand up that day in July, 1988 after losing my son's case, walk to the train station, and peacefully go home.

YOUR MENTAL HEALTH IS ROOTED IN YOUR HISTORY

Your mental health is rooted in historical events: what your parents, grandparents, and great-grandparents experienced as well as the events of our ancestors going back thousands of years. We all carry an ancestral karma, an inner code of the souls of our ancestors (Farmer, 2014). The collective unconscious contains the emotional spirits of our ancestors (Boeree, 2009). The collective unconscious can go beyond the time of our immediate ancestors. Our spiritual ancestors can go back more than a thousand years and, for some, more than millions of years (Farmer, 2014).

Many Africans, the first humans, who came to America, had immediate and spiritual ancestors who had been pharaohs, shamans, social reformers, builders, spiritual healers, kings, emperors, tribal chiefs, queens, princes, and princesses (Clarke, 1993). After being forced into America, they may have had "masters" whose histories were full of killers, rapists, conquerors, adventurers, and belief in genocide as entertainment. Years of this historic dynamic affected the social brain and mental health of many humans. For social brain healing, we need ancestral veneration.

Ancient ancestral veneration is practiced in some cultures. It's about honoring our ancestors, immediate or spiritual, respecting them, and maintaining their teachings in our spiritual wise mind. Some ancestors may have done cruel and hurtful acts, nonetheless you can be released from those behaviors by sending an energy force of love and kindness to that ancestor for healing, and you become the healer of that hurtful energy (Farmer, 2014).

The child *within* has the inner history, which is rooted in historical events that happened to our parents and grandparents, and how the history of the world was told. We all have the mother *within*, the father *within*, the community *within*, the spiritual ancestor *within*, and the child *within*. These *withins* create neural synapses—brain connections and neurochemical energy or neurotransmitters that charges the nervous system. Your spiritual *withins*, your historical *withins*, and your current *withins* may be affecting your level of emotional vulnerability.

For example, during slavery times in the 1600s to the 1900s, African Americans were unable to obtain an education; it was against the law for us to learn how to read. When I met my client John in the year 2004, he had the belief that Black people were not into being educated, not into doing homework, reading from a book, or working hard in a classroom to get an "A." John followed a stereotype for being Black; educated Blacks who were their own natural self were acting White, and Black males who articulated English well were gay. These labels of Black and White affected his brain neural activity that was passed down from one generation. John's mother and father were both drug addicted and unable to raise their children, most likely due to the psychological impact of ancestral karma. They both lived with the divide and conquer *within*, which was now a part of John's "*within* system." He was definitely on the path of having children without marrying and without financially supporting them, without being physically present to assure the future of his offspring and to commit to a life of family first. This is not possible if you have an unresolved divide and conquer within. Your brain is simply not programmed to love and honor spouse and children. John's *within* experiences led to a social brain that was ripe for absolute failure and long-term imprisonment, which was the *within* of slavery and the Jim Crow community.

How did my great-grandfather, born in the 1800s, and a slave during slavery and Jim Crow times, manage to earn a master's degree and become a minister able to teach about spiritual capitalism, while John, born in the 1990s, thought that being Black meant not being interested in achieving high academic standards? Many of the slave community may have been more in touch with their spiritual ancestry than people are today. Europeans are more connected to their spiritual ancestors than people of African descent. Many people of African descent are totally unaware of an African named **Imhotep.** He may have been the world's first multi-genius, and he has been referred to as the father of medicine. Besides medicine, he was the architect of the Great Pyramid in Africa (Clarke, 1993). Imhotep was also a spiritual healer who used prayer, peace (meditation), and positive thinking. He believed that we are visitors on the planet and should contribute to the "merriment" of the world. This was before Jesus Christ (2980 B.C.) (Clarke, 1993, p. 24).

Slavery was not simply a failure community or a victim community; it could also be a humane community. In ancient Africa, slavery was more humane; "slaves were known to rise above their servitude and become kings" (Clarke, 1993, p. 53). The law of Moses states "if a man smite his servant or his maid with a rod, and he dies under his hand he shall be surely punished" (Clarke, 1993, p. 53). Slaves had dignity it was those who beat, oppressed, raped that lacked dignity, but they were wealthy.

In modern America, the purpose of slavery was to dehumanize. Nonetheless, it taught many how to survive in a community under the most horrible of conditions. Survival became a part of the emotional journey for African people, and also for non-African people, for many Europeans were also enslaved. In the slave community of survival, many individuals of all ethnic groups performed heroic acts for the sake of freedom and a pursuit of happiness for all members of the human family. They had visions beyond and above the negativity of the dominant, narcissistic civilization. They had visions that created positive emotions and found a way of life for healing and contributing to their community.

HUMAN STRATEGIES FROM OUR SPIRITUAL ANCESTORS

In this chapter, you can learn from great leaders, your spiritual ancestors. To have a social brain healing it is important to celebrate and venerate your ethnicity. Knowing your ethnic heritage can have a healing impact. Since we all have African ancestors, we all can benefit from the spiritual ancestors you will read about in this chapter. You may not have heard of them from the perspective of how they managed to withstand the effects of traumatic stress or retaliatory stress. Their stories, like that of our spiritual ancestor, **Imhotep**, show the power of prayer, peace, loving kindness, education, and healing, which can provide a foundation for managing and healing your own traumatic or retaliatory stress.

The stories of the spiritual ancestors can provide the tools and human strategies to help you reduce your own emotional vulnerability. Their stories can teach you that violence and rage are not solutions that lead to success. Rage and violence cannot help you make positive contributions to your family, your community, and to the human race.

My great-grandfather Promise Mayfield, born in Virginia as a slave—he was a survivor. I never met him, but I heard his story. He experienced a great deal of pain but maintained his mental health and his happiness. Unfortunately, many of the mental health contributions of great old Americans during slavery and Jim Crow were not passed down and incorporated in our American culture. This chapter seeks to bring to life those human strategies that may originate in and have survival roots from the ancestors of us all, the first modern humans of Africa.

Use these skills for emotional regulation during horrible times; for coping with traumatic stress, when faced with extreme challenges; and for beginning your journey to make positive contributions to non-violence, progressive mental health, happiness, and loving kindness to others.

Human strategies are based on ethnotherapy theories (Anderson, 1983). Ethnotherapy was first developed in the early 1970s by Dr. Price Cobbs, who also co-wrote the book *Black Rage (Grier & Cobbs, 2000)*. Basically, ethnotherapy sees a strong relationship between the *withins* of spiritual life, community life, ethnic culture, and emotional stability (Anderson, 1983). The historical withins such as the Jim Crow American community for many Americans have a wealth of survival information that is not shared in the light of improving mental health and happiness.

An old American is an American whose family history go back to the 1600s and the first thirteen colonies. These are Americans of Indian descent, of African descent, and of European descent. Many people want to forget that historical community when America was in its infancy stage. However, we all need to accept and to own that oppression; racism; and cruel, violent behaviors did exist, and that the emotionally traumatic impact continues on in the social brains of many Americans and non-Americans today. Nonetheless, there also were those like my great-grandfather Promise Mayfield, thumb-suckers who sought peace and promoted love, spirituality, and support of others.

The human strategies are a way to help you gain coping strategies and learn from those individuals who had painful experiences just like those you are having today. They survived without the support systems that exist now. Many of these individuals did not even have the support of biological family due to the concept of divide-and-conquer laws. Divide and conquer meant separating husband and wife and children for a lifetime. The mother would be sold in one area, the father in another area, and the children could be divided and sold in totally different areas.

ON BOARD A SLAVE-SHIP.

Africans forced to American and brain programmed for failure with Divide and Conquer.

It is empowering to know your ethnic heritage and such knowledge will contribute to positive mental health. The uniqueness about the Africans was they were the first modern humans and they had a civilization based on a kinship, and love for all life forms. They were not xenophobic or hateful. It is important for all Americans, because we all have an African ancestor, to give a salute and venerate old African Americans who had painful experiences; many brutally removed from their biological parents, but they found positive ways to enhance their self-esteem, survive, and contribute in a positive way without retaliation to America and to the planet. Their brains tapped into the legacy of knowledge of the first modern humans for survival, learning, and kinship with all life forms.

1. **Dr. Booker T. Washington** was born a slave in 1856, yet he earned a doctoral degree. He knew the pangs of hunger and oppression, yet he always had a quest for knowledge about the events around him. At fifteen, he left home to work for his education at the Hampton Institute. He became a teacher and held classes for children during the day and for adults at night. When he was only twenty-one years old, he founded Tuskegee Institute, which emphasized industrial and agricultural education. In today's language, that would translate to providing majors in mining engineering; agricultural engineering; and civil engineering. Dr. Washington felt that the key to success was education, by any means possible along with hard work. His institute became a training center for old Americans of African descent to become teachers, ministers, and farmers, and to inspire individuals to believe in themselves and to work towards self-improvement especially in the fields of industrial and agricultural engineering. He did not espouse acts of aggression and retaliation; in fact, he was very much against such actions.

The Washington Skill: Booker T. Washington was a great leader. He stated that political agitation and rage against the inequalities of racism would *not* save people of color. The Washington Skill concerns the ability to own; to learn; to develop industrial skills like engineering; to have knowledge of economics; to value the possibilities of freedom and spiritual capitalism; to acquire intellectual skills and enhance your PFC; and to honor with a developed PFC the history of ancestors who fought for freedom, justice, and true democracy. **The Washington Skill** does not include aggression or criminal acts. The Washington Skill tells you to study what you don't know or to study and be the best at what you do know. If there are no medical doctors in your family, consider becoming a medical doctor. If there are no pilots in your family, consider becoming a pilot. Strive for education, diversified education, such as the sciences, law (if you want to fight for civil rights and justice, study law and graduate with honors). Study engineering, architecture, agriculture, and medicine. The Washington Skill requires that you aim for the highest grade possible. Be an advocate of objective tests rather than the subjective decisions that come from a teacher's or professor's opinion of your ability or work.

Dr. Booker T. Washington was instrumental in starting a university during a time when pain and suffering were rampant. Progressive mental health and happiness is something you must work at. No one will give it to you; you must do your own work. You may be locked in a prison, but you can begin your spiritual journey towards progressive happiness and mental health anywhere. Start with the Serenity Prayer; know the three minds—emotional, rational, and wise. Tap into your brain for the wise mind and say No to fighting, and develop your PFC.

2. George W. Carver was born a slave in 1864. He was a frail and sickly boy, but he had goals. His chief goal was to go to college and to learn all he could about plant life. Life was not easy for Mr. Carver. From grade school to college, he had to work very hard to earn money to continue his schooling. He graduated college and contributed to the field of agriculture, making it possible to produce better crops and create better living for all people. Later in life, he was a friend to Henry Ford and an advisor to scientists throughout the world. As a result of his discoveries, new industries were started and new jobs were made available for many workers.

The Carver Skill: Learn to self-heal. Set goals, even if you are sickly or have a learning disability. Tell yourself you can achieve that goal and do not focus on the barriers. You may be challenged in some way, but if you set a goal and work hard, you will see positive results and know that you did the best that you could. The main idea of the Carver Skill is to set goals for yourself. You will be amazed by what you can achieve. Do not make excuses or focus on the negative.

3. Frederick Douglass was born a slave in Maryland in 1817. Douglass never knew his father or his mother. He learned about his mother just before she died. As a child he was hungry, cold and had a harsh life. When he was eight he was sent from the Maryland plantation to the city Baltimore to work as a servant and a shipyard laborer. As a young boy, he spent most of his spare time improving his reading skills. He did receive help from the lady of the house who was told by her husband that what she was doing was against the law. After learning the basis of ABC's, he worked very hard at it; he had a **goal** that he would learn to read, and read well. When he was twenty-one, he ran away from the South and went north to escape the shackles of slavery. Can you imagine what his life was like while he was on the run? Far worse than the quality of life for most prisoners today, who get three meals, a bed to sleep on, visitors, and commissary. Nonetheless, he had the goals and the motivation, which developed the prefrontal cortex (PFC) of his brain, and he became a popular speaker against oppression and the evilness of slavery.

Mr. Douglass settled in New York, where he started and published the newspaper, "North Star." Today, some Americans, who were born free in this country, are unable to read a newspaper, let alone able to start and publish a newspaper—like my client John. During and after the Civil War, Mr. Douglass served and contributed to America as an advisor, public official, and minister to Haiti. He found a way to make a positive contribution to society. His twenty-one room colonial-style house in Anacostia, D.C., has been made a national shrine.

The Douglass Skill: Read and improve your ability to communicate about injustice and listen to opinions that you may not agree with. Improve your emotional vulnerability to opinions that you do not agree with. You can practice the Douglass Skill for conflict resolution with your partner or spouse. Sit down and let one person speak while the other listens for about fifteen minutes. The Douglass Skill is a profound understanding about conflict and resolving conflict without violence. Tap into the part of your brain geared towards peace or begin to develop a neural synapse for conflict resolution without hate or rage. When there is conflict, there are two sides; don't aggressively attack the other person. Keep your conversation focused on the issue. Learn to breathe deeply and communicate with your wise mind, not your emotional mind or rational mind that thinks you have a right to aggressively attack someone. Learn to resolve conflict without violence or harm to the other person using your **Douglass Skill** of communication.

4. Robert Smalls was born a slave in 1839. He was forced to work as a deck hand on the Confederate Navy ship, the Planter. Instead of feeling sorry for himself in this forced position, he learned all he could about it. He paid attention to every detail. His ability to accept his situation coupled with his ability to pay attention to the many details on the Navy ship allowed for advanced development of his prefrontal cortex. Ultimately, he was able to gain freedom for himself and his family. He later served as a river pilot and rose to the rank of captain. After the Civil War was over, Mr. Smalls served in the House of Representatives from 1875-1887 and in the Senate of South Carolina. Throughout his life, he promoted civil rights for all people. He had that innate neural synapse for a kinship with all humans.

The Smalls Skill is to do your best even if you start at the bottom. I knew a woman who worked as a maid and saved all her money. Her employer always complimented her work, and she always aimed to do the best she could. Eventually, she saved enough to start her own cleaning business, which was profitable. Sometimes, doing your best on the job may not be recognized, but don't look at the negative. Remember, some humans are purely ego-centered and are unable to see your value, only theirs. See the bigger picture for yourself, whether you are a maid or a vice president of a company.

The Smalls Skill is to learn all you can; it doesn't matter what your position is. If your workplace offers to contribute towards employee education, take advantage of it. That is something positive about the world you live in, and you deserve the benefits.

5. Jan Matzeliger was born a free African American in 1852. He worked many years as an apprentice to a shoemaker in Philadelphia and then settled in Lynn, Massachusetts, where he worked in a shoe factory. He was a hard worker and paid close attention to the highly skilled men who finished the shoes by sewing the uppers to the soles of the shoes by hand. After ten years of close observation, he built a machine that could attach the upper to the sole of the shoe and do it as well as a man could. The machine turned out four hundred pairs of shoes in one day, whereas skilled workers had turned out only forty pairs a day. This invention by Mr. Matzeliger caused shoe production to leap from one million to eleven million pairs a year. Jan Matzeliger received a patent on the machine in 1883, but after Matzeliger's death, the United Shoe Machinery Company took over his patent. Machines based on Mr. Matzeliger's invention are used throughout the world.

The Matzeliger Skill: Be an inventor; develop a talent you may not be aware that you have. You may have just lost your job, but today you can try to do some kind of work, even volunteer work. Your ability to work moves you towards normalcy and increases the PFC. Be grateful and thankful for the work you have. Pay close attention. Your job may be sweeping floors at McDonalds, but if you are grateful to have it and thankful, you could one day own a McDonald's franchise or start your own food chain by using the Matzeliger Skill to pay attention to the details of your job.

6. Paul Cuffe was born 1759. His father was from the Ashanti Empire in West Africa. He was born a free African American and became a shipbuilder and ship-owner. He was a successful Massachusetts merchant during the colonial period in American history. He went to sea at age sixteen, and a few years later, he was building his own ships. In 1780, with other free African Americans, he protested the right of the government to make him pay taxes while denying his right to vote. By 1811, he was the wealthiest African American in the United States.

Mr. Cuffe was a pioneer for his loving kinship acts of humanitarianism and philanthropy. He used his own money so that African American children could get an education. He believed in the importance of establishing cultural relations with the motherland,

Africa and doing what could be done to help modernized the motherland Africa. He also provided funds and transportation for African Americans who wanted to return to Africa, especially to Sierra Leone. Cuffe, with other African Americans, established The Friendly Society of Sierra Leone, a trading organization run by African Americans who had returned to West Africa with goals of financial enterprise and modernization.

The Cuffe Skill is for anyone who is fortunate enough to be financially well-off. Help children in less fortunate areas gain a sound education and have an opportunity to experience a fun-land, with rides, a circus, and games. All children should laugh and have a fun-land to go to. I can say that Oprah Winfrey is an example of someone who has been a great humanitarian to viewers of her show, giving gifts of cars and trips to different countries. She also started a school in South Africa for girls. Prime Minister Tayyip Erdogan of Turkey has been a great leader in humanitarian efforts for education in Somalia and Ethiopia. He encourages advanced education for citizens in these African countries which will yield long-term benefits. The organization The Giving Pledge fosters humanitarian efforts by Americans Warren Buffet, Mark Zuckerberg, and Bill and Melinda Gates; these current humanitarian efforts all demonstrate what the Cuffe Skill is all about.

7. Mary McLeod Bethune, born 1875, became a teacher, a public speaker, and a governmental administrator. She devoted her entire life to bringing dignity, opportunity, and hope to old Americans of color. She worked hard and saved by doing many different jobs, earning enough money so she could start a school for girls in the Daytona Beach, Florida, area. In 1923, the Bethune School joined with the Cookman Institute to become Bethune-Cookman College.

President Franklin D. Roosevelt appointed Mrs. Bethune to serve as the director of the Negro Affairs Division of the National Youth Administration. Both President and Mrs. Roosevelt were great admirers of old American Mary McLeod Bethune. She was given the Spingarn Medal for Negro Achievement in the year 1935.

The Bethune Skill: When I was a child, I attended a private school in Harlem for one year. My teacher there told me the importance of the Bethune Skill. Have dignity, do not use profanity, speak clearly, and make eye contact. Develop and encourage dignity and spiritual growth. If you are a teacher, the skill is to be creative and develop new ways to motivate your students to get the highest grades possible.

8. Phillis Wheatley was kidnapped from Africa at the age of nine and brought to America as a slave. She served as a maid to a family that gave her their name. The family loved her. When she became ill, the Wheatley family took her to England so she could receive the best of care. Ms. Wheatley enjoyed writing and her adopted family encouraged her to do so. During the time she spent in England, she wrote some of her early poetry. Her first book of poems was published in London in 1773. She is one the better known poets of the colonial period in American history.

The Wheatley Skill: Develop your writing ability. If you have a message or a talent, bring it out in music, books, and poems for the entire human race to enjoy. Develop relationships with a variety of people. Goodness exists in our human family. Find ways to tap into it to bring joy to yourself and to others.

9. Norbert Rillieux was born a slave in New Orleans in 1806. He was a highly intelligent boy. Rillieux was fortunate that his master had a humane kinship neural synapse and recognized that he was gifted. He arranged for him to get a college education in France, where he studied engineering. He worked in a sugar-refining plant and learned all that he could. Norbert invented the Rillieux machines that improved the method of evaporation and speeded it up so that sugar could be extracted at a lower cost. Eventually, this machine was used in all tropical lands where sugarcane was grown. Today, the Rillieux process is also used in making condensed milk, soap, gelatin, and glue.

The Rillieux Skill: Innovate and create. Study engineering, and pay close attention in your classes. The Africans were the first human inventors; first, they built libraries, and then they built the pyramids (Jackson, 1970). This ancestry skill for innovation and creative energy may be within you. You will not tap into it if your mind/brain is filled with anger, retaliatory stress, and rage.

10. Richard Allen was born a slave in 1760. He worked very hard, day and night, eventually earning two thousand dollars to buy his freedom. He became skilled as a scientist, creative writer, and organizer, but what shaped his career was the prejudices and discrimination of overt narcissists. He was a thumb-sucker and did not respond with retaliation or with covert narcissism, but found ways to enhance his community and contribute to the PFC development of others. He became the first old American of color or I prefer the first Nubian to organize his people around self-help programs. In 1794, he and other African Americans started the first Independent African American church. By 1816, he had established a national organization for the African Methodist Episcopal Church and was chosen its first bishop.

The Allen Skill leads to activities that provide spiritual and emotional growth for others/self-help. I am using the Allen Skill to write this book.

11. Lewis Latimer was born to a poor Boston family in 1848; his parents had escaped from slavery in Virginia and migrated to Boston, but his father was hunted as a fugitive, and eventually he disappeared. To help support his family, young Latimer worked hard selling newspapers. In 1864, at the age of sixteen, Latimer lied about his age and was able to enlist in the United States Navy. He received an honorable discharge for his efforts in the Civil War. He obtained a job in a patent law office. Latimer was talented. By observing others, he taught himself mechanical drawing and drafting. Latimer designed a number of inventions, including an improved railroad car bathroom and an early air conditioning unit.

The Latimer Skill: Study engineering and strive to invent. Even before the twentieth century, many old Americans of African descent had patented hundreds of inventions. These old Americans of color invented things despite lack of recognition and despite the hate and discrimination they had to endure. Among those old Americans Nubians whose inventions helped the United States was Mr. Latimer. During his lifetime, he worked with both Alexander Graham Bell and Thomas Edison.

12. Dr. Martin Luther King, Jr., was born in 1929. He received his doctorate degree at Boston University in 1955 and later formed the Southern Christian Leadership Conference. Dr. King sought social action and change for African Americans based on a Christian philosophy and practices of non-violence. He believed that violence leads to destruction and ultimately to more violence. Dr. King had traumatic experiences of pain, but he believed in strong character and in activities that strengthen the PFC, such as advanced education. Dr. King gained fame throughout the world for his efforts to end social injustices by means of non-violence. He was awarded the Nobel

Peace Prize in 1964. Under his leadership, people from all groups who also wanted to eliminate social injustices, oppression, racism, and violence came together. When Dr. King was assassinated in 1968, he was mourned by people of all groups throughout the world. Dr. King was a believer in non-violence in a world that was consumed by hate and violence.

The Dr. King Skill: Say No to injustice, using non-violent methods. Be mindful that individuals who cause pain and trauma come in tailored suits, in police uniforms, as professors with PhDs, and as doctors with MDs, but when they are in positions of authority, especially police learn to be humble. Evil people are not all drug dealers, thieves, or rapists. You can use the Dr. King Skill for non-violent ways to fight injustice. Participate peacefully in marches against injustice. Write about your experiences with injustice and how you overcame the pain and suffering. Using the Dr. King Skill, you can contribute non-violently to the advancement of your community. You may not always be successful, but in the process, you will build strong character and improve your progressive mental health. Use words to assert your message but not to hurt those who may have caused you pain.

Be on the side of the advancement of the human family seeking to venerate the first modern humans who were peaceful and survived several hundred thousand years ago. We could be extinct like the dinosaurs, but the modern human who originated in Africa lives on in us all, today. There is a woman who currently lives in the south, she is African American. She did a search of her family tree using DNA and discovered that her ancestry goes as far back as 338,000.00 years ago based on an A00 Y chromosomes of a male relative. Bring non-violence into your life and the life of your family and venerate the first modern humans for survival of the happiness hormones that we inherited, that allows us to be humble and non-violent, but at times we fail to use.

13. Madam C. J. Walker was born on a plantation in 1867. Both of her parents were slaves, and by age seven, she was an orphan (a victim of divide and conquer). She worked as a laborer in the cotton fields of Mississippi. In her own words: "I am a woman who came from the cotton fields of the South. From there I was promoted to the wash tub; from there to the kitchen; and from there, I promoted myself!"

She also wrote, "There is no royal flower strewn path to success. And if there is, I have not found it, for whatever success I have attained has been the result of much hard work and many sleepless nights" (Walker, 1912).

Madam Walker was the first female in America to become a self-made millionaire. There were American females of European descent who had inherited millions, but Madam Walker was the first female who, strictly through her own sweat and tears, became a self-made millionaire in America. She developed and marketed beauty and hair products.

Years later, after becoming a business woman by using her PFC and wise mind, Madam C. J. Walker provided training and inspiration to more than two hundred women—many who had been maids, cooks, and sharecroppers. They assembled in Philadelphia with the goal of becoming women entrepreneurs. Walker gave prizes not only to the agents who had sold the most products, but also to those individuals in her woman's group who had contributed the most to charity. This woman's group spoke out against lynching and the need for it to be a federal crime. Can you imagine, you could lynch and kill someone and not have consequences.

The Madame Walker Skill is specifically for females. Discover your physical beauty. Enhance your outer beauty. Having short, kinky hair or curly hair is a humanoid feature. Hairiness and straight hair is less of a humanoid feature. However, today, being hairy is very popular. Add color and keep your hair neat and clean. You can also embrace something popular in our culture, the long hair styles. The Madame Walker skill is for beauty, outer beauty as well as inner beauty. Madame Walker encouraged her employees to pay attention to injustices and to give to charities. Madame Walker said, "Love your country, America."

14. Nelson Mandela: Although not born in America, he suffered in the same way as individuals who were born into slavery, or those first humans who spent centuries trying to escape the brutalities of genocide and oppression in East Africa. His bad experience was Apartheid in South Africa.

The Mandela Skill: Life is full of pain, but you can always build a beautiful and successful garden (Stengel, 2010). You can plant that garden in your mind, in your brain. Keep it growing, and keep the brain de-cluttered of hate, revenge, and rage. Find peace and leave a legacy of loving kind-heartedness for others to learn from.

15. Marcus A. Garvey: The history of the old African American is forced immigration. Garvey, a great Nubian leader, believed in the survival of the African race, the first humans. He encouraged African Americans to maintain African culture and return to Africa to help with African modernization. Africa is the motherland of us all; humans have an African ancestor and roots in the African motherland.

The Garvey Skill is to know **the truth of your** genealogical history, know your ethnic history, and your ties to the first modern humans of Africa, find ways to venerate your ancestors. We as humans survived because of totemism a way of life of the first modern humans of Africa. Venerate not for the sake of separation based of differences, but for human relativeness. In our current world, promote the kinship and loving kindness that is a humanoid characteristic. Garvey would say read, read and read. Learn, learn and learn; strengthen Africa for its centuries of persecution and hardship; remember the sufferings of the forefathers venerate them with your success (Garvey, 2004).

The information on the Americans obtained at http://www.biography.com. These individuals embodied the true human spirit, the kinship spirit of the first humans, the Africans.

USE THE HUMAN SKILLS OF YOUR ANCESTORS TO REPROGRAM YOUR BRAIN

To my readers, you can rewire and reprogram the neural circuits and pathways of your brain to create a lifestyle of non-violence, loving kindness towards others, mental health success and happiness for yourself. In a world of narcissists where bad things will happen, you can be the positive energy and spiritual force for peace and love. Do not allow the evilness of others to create large deposits of anger and rage, which will impact your mental and physical health. You must be a warrior for your own happiness and keep the happy hormones alive in your brain.

The history of the first African humans was shaped with kinship and loving kindness towards thy neighbor. Boys respected men because any man could be their father; girls respected women because any woman could be their mother. If you have poor anger management, depression, anxiety, failure in your work or your love life, social phobias, financial problems, feelings of hopelessness, or just a lack of happiness in your life, take a moment and think is your life, your visit to the planet. Is it worse off than those who suffered in the 1600s to the 1800s? Imagine the first humans and their culture of a kinship with all life. Identify with your first ancestors and begin to cultivate what is good about your life, and what you can be grateful for.

Using imagery you can follow the teachings of great old Americans who survived pain, suffering, discrimination and poverty. Tell their stories of survival and success over and over again or sit quietly and imagine their human strategy for success. What will be your human strategies that you can pass on to others? Imagine your spiritual ancestors overcoming barriers and see yourself doing the same. In this way your brain can form social neural pathways for healing. Imagine coping with life without rage. What constructive steps will you take? Forgive yourself if you have made mistakes; your brain was programmed to make mistakes. Forgive others so that the deposits of anger and rage are not impacting the neurobiology of your brain. With forgiveness you can have positive goals, hope, the ability to cross any barrier, and you will keep the happy hormones alive in your brain.

The human strategies are important for children, as well. In fact, the human strategies provide inspiration for all people. While working at the children's hospital, a married Caucasian couple told me on the first day of their visit to the hospital that their teenage son would not talk to me and could I arrange for him to have another therapist. Their son was aggressive, violent, a bully, and prone to hate. His parents were followers of the KKK and Aryan teachings.

I explained the policy of the hospital: for the first eleven days I would have to complete my assessment, and if their son wanted another therapist, I would arrange it with the treatment team. After eleven days, the parents returned, expecting that their son would be getting a new therapist. During my sessions and interventions with their son, I had taught him the **Dr. King Skill** of non-violence and building character. The boy told his parents that he felt the treatment at the hospital was helping him, and that he did not want to change therapists.

He did well and advanced in our treatment program for non-violence and kinship towards others. He was not sent back home, but was sent to a diverse residential school so that he could learn to live with different members of the human family. He did well. A year later, the parents were again at the hospital with their younger son. This time, at admission, they wanted their younger son to work with me.

HEAL YOURSELF WITH ETHNOTHERAPY AND ANCESTRAL REGRESSION:

Ethnotherapy allows you to connect your dots to world history, your ancestral inheritance, and seeks to change negative attitudes. Ethnotherapy skills are based on the principles of the successful survival of old Americans and their ancestral connection to the first humans. You can tap into the positive energy of mother earth and the first humans. They had an intelligence of the human spirit, which allowed for the survival of the first modern humans despite horrific and harsh conditions. Ethnotherapy and ancestral regressions can strengthen your brain and your prefrontal cortex, if you can become mindful of their emotional strategies and incorporate the emotional intelligence of the first human spirit for your own healing. When you are in states of rage and retaliation, you weaken your brain's ability to be inventive and to thrive for success and happiness. Yes, life is full of pain, that is one of the realities of the world that you live in, but don't be a victim. Know that even though the world is unfair, cruel, and causes pain, *you* can have the courage to contribute to your community and your world for the sake of kinship with all life forms and loving kindness.

Start by healing yourself. Stop repeating in your mind that you cannot do something. Stop believing that something is beyond your grasp. Strive for financial independence and start saving now; one dollar a day, if that is what you have. The **Allen Skill** is about saving money for your future. In the 1700s, he worked very hard, day and night, to earn two thousand dollars to buy his freedom. Today, you will work hard and save for the sake of your progressive happiness and for your progressive mental health. The earlier you start the better. Find out if your job provides ways for you to save money. There is something called "Deferred Comp," in which money is taken from your weekly income and invested. Striving to achieve the goal of financial success does wonders for the brain. It stimulates the happy hormones—endorphins, dopamine, and serotonin.

If people block you, don't let it destroy who you are. Start down another road to success. Smile and laugh. By working hard to achieve industrial skills, business skills, and social skills; or, if you are so inclined, discover and develop your talent and make it work for you as an entrepreneur or some creative task. In the late 1700s, Paul Cuffe was building his own ships. During a time in world history when laws were developed to prevent Nubians from learning to read. By 1811, Cuffe was the wealthiest African American in the United States. Mr. Cuffe was also a pioneer for loving kinship in acts of humanitarianism and philanthropy. Do you think life was easy for him? No. So, use the **Cuffe Skill**.

Booker T. Washington stated that political agitation and rage against the inequalities of racism will *not* save you. Use the **Washington Skill** to let go of revenge and forgive others. See what beauty there is in the world and contribute towards that beauty. Americans have the ability to live without revenge and retaliation. Value the possibilities of spiritual capitalism, which is based on the helping-hand theory of capitalism that your success leads to the success of others. Acquire intellectual skills, honor and value family, like Madame Walker said, despite her struggles, "Love your country, America." These human strategies of your spiritual ancestors have roots that reach back to the ancient African age of totemism, which is needed for happiness and progressive mental health.

Start your healing today for the sake of your happiness and progressive mental health.

- Accept the true reality of world history and our relatedness as a human family, we are all cousins.
- Self-Emotional-Evolution is shown in your ability to love your neighbor as you love yourself, which is rooted in Ancient African teachings, but be a modern day totemism—that all life is a related part of divine nature.
- You can incorporated the ancient African teaching and venerate the ancestors whose spirits were for peace loving kindness with others. When you are free of hate, envy, greed, violence, rage, and victim mentality, then you can incorporate a modern day totemism and evolve. Stop being a victim. Has your life been worse than your ancestor Nelson Mandela, who spent 27 years in prison and denied all rights in his

native country or Madam C. J. Walker, who was orphaned as a child? Even if it has been worse, do as they did, have a constructive goal. Don't become a victim become a success story. With social brain healing, you can.

HEAL YOURSELF WITH ETHNOTHERAPY AND 5 DOORS FOR ANCESTRAL REGRESSION:

The social brain is like an I-Pad with many APPs that started at conception, before you were born, with your parent's temperament and their ancestral inheritance. These APPs create neural synapse for healing or for suffering. You can begin the process to delete the APPs that cause suffering for you and for others. You may be locked up in a prison, but today, think of Nelson Mandela, let him be your spiritual ancestor, sit quietly, relax all the muscles in your body with deep breaths in and slowly out for peace, serenity and calmness. Imagine seeing 5 doors:

Door 1, Your immediate or adopted family. Do a family tree in your calming journal, which consist of your mother, father, grandparents, and great grandparents on each side. Visualize the life they had or if adopted visualize the life of the biological parent based on a world view. Was it finances, religion, being too young, or demands from others that led to the adoption? The beauty is you are having a visit on the planet, wow!!

Door 2, Distant family (e.g. those in slavery times) those from Africa, Europe, Asia.

Door 3, First human door (Africans go back thousands or millions of years). In this door you can bring a piece of African artifact or recall documentaries such as Dr. Spencer Wells, Journey of man: A genetic odyssey or create an altar that represents totemism-a modern day kinship with all life forms. This alter is for your visualization and to honor the struggles of the first humans, the Africans. The first humans' beginning life led to the survival of the human world we have today.

Develop and encourage dignity and spiritual growth, to venerate the first humans by becoming humanoid, non-violent, the ta-merrian way, a kinship with other humans as your brother, sister or cousin. No matter where you are today, you can start to heal and contribute to the world that you live in, using the thumb-sucking, ta-merrian, and humanoid way of the evolved spiritual energies for kinship. Know that your brain is your greatest asset and use it to create thoughts that will heal towards self and global transformation of loving kindness.

Door 4, Human hybrid family, we all share an ancestor so we are cousins; but our human journey has led to cultural mistrust and the inability to love thy neighbor. This can be a healing door for all members of the human family.

Door 5, Your spiritual ancestor door, someone you admire, someone you know who triumphed over significant pain and suffering, but with a level of dignity, someone like Nelson Mandela.

All the doors can be used via guided imagery/visualization for coping with anger and rage in a healthy way so that you increase heathy neuro-chemicals in your mind and body. Use the doors for forgiveness; use the doors to transform negative emotions towards self and others into loving kindness; use the doors so you can live in peace; and use the doors to contribute to the ending of rage, the ending of the exploding volcano of hate and retaliation that spreads negative energy and impacts everyone.

Let's try *Door #5* which for this exercise will be the Nelson Mandela skill. First, before you start, it is important to know what is causing you stress and anger. What are your symptoms? Some people yell, curse, and fight; others hide in their room; some people over eat, drink too much alcohol, use drugs; others may isolate and call out sick from work. Let's say that your stress is: A Toxic Supervisor. You will sit in a quiet or peaceful place:

See all 5 doors but today you will walk through Door 5 and see Mr. Mandela, he will be your advisor in this ancestral regression process. With your eyes closed: look towards door # 5, when you open the door imagine you are greeted with a smile by Mr. Mandela. What is he wearing; is his hair cut short; how does he speak. Are you in Africa, what are your surroundings like (visualize a place)? You will tell him what you know about him and asked how he managed 27 years in prison and later became the president of his country and ended apartheid. You will tell him about your stressors and your symptoms. What will he tell you, what healing words might he suggest? He responds: *you must build a garden for peace, take care of something or someone, have goals, forgive for your own mental*

health, see the good in your world, and find ways to contribute to that energy of goodness.

If you spiritual ancestor is Mary McLeod Bethune, use the door to start the **Bethune skill.** You can start your neural pathway for dignity. Commit for 30 days to not use profanity, speak clearly, remove clutter from your home, and end rage in your life with a partner or on the job or with your children. Honor your spiritual ancestor for 30 days or more.

After seeing your spiritual ancestor in your positive imagined thoughts; say words of affirmation that will heal: my supervisor has baggage, is he or she narcissistic? If so, I have no control over that social illness. I will go to work on time and complete all my assignments. If I'm being abused or harassed, I will talk to someone; and seek legal advice, if necessary. Continue to sit in a meditative position, eyes close. Take deep breaths in and out and say the words taken from Buddhist teachings (Jennings. 2010) to yourself for developing the loving kindness APP in your brain:

May I be happy. May I be healthy. May I be safe. May I be peaceful. May I live with ease.

Say this for (1) yourself, (2) someone you love, (3) a neutral person (4) a hostile person (your toxic supervisor).

For example: imagine a hostile person in your life or the toxic supervisor, see that person and say "may this hostile person be happy, may this hostile person be healthy, may this hostile person be peaceful, may this hostile person live with ease (this will not be easy to do, but with social brain healing, you will be better able to forgive).

Start your calming journal, list your painful APPs, and list your grateful APPs. You can begin DNA extractions, by deleting negative

APPs that lead to fight, flight, or lack of empathy towards others or an inability to be humble. You can delete the APP that leads to criminal behaviors or fights with your spouse or partner. A negative APP might also be an alcoholic father who hit you. Delete those behaviors of hitting and fighting; acknowledge that they did happen. Know your father's history; was he neglected, abused, or did his ethnic history contribute to his negative APPs that you inherited and/or experienced. Show empathy for that father and forgive.

Transcend being id-centered. Reflect on your ancestors and the history of abuse within the human family. Reflect on the story of the lynching of Arthur Steven in 1933, whose side of the story is your ancestor? Know that not all Europeans would have supported lynching. Many Europeans have the DNA pathway for a kinship with all life forms. There is the movie which is a true story of Solomon Northup who was a free Nubian in 1841, living in New York, but he was kidnapped and forced into slavery on a cotton plantation (Meltzer, 1964). He was beaten and abused yet he maintained his dignity and there were Europeans who helped in a loving kindness manner. The movie is Twelve Years a Slave. Because of divide and conquer or other Jim Crow laws, your dad may have lacked dignity, you can visualize your father being healed, and you can forgive.

Once you have acknowledged and placed your *withins* as part of the concept of world history, and ancestral history, you are now ready to delete. You will know that unhealthy APPs have been deleted when you are no longer struck in denial, anger, rage, anxiety, depression or hate. And you may cross off that APP. You may heal emotionally, but you may be left with addictions.

Your chance of ending unhealthy addictions to drugs, for example, is far greater now with social brain healing. If you have more positive APPs in your mind, you will be able to live with ease. A positive brain APP might result from a spouse who tells you every day "I love you" and gives you a hug; be grateful for that APP and smile and do the same for your partner. Remember that social brain healing is cultivating positive thoughts that heal. Positive thoughts can reprogram your brain for progressive happiness and progressive mental health. Remember Energy =mc² we can't create new energy, but we can change energy from one form to another (Farmer, 2014). You as an individual can begin the journey and contribute to the changing of the energy from the form that contributes to the volcano of hate, rage, violence and retaliation to the energy form that contributes to loving kindness. Also know, and this is very important, racism, hate, and violence these are all indications of a social mental illness, you cannot correct the mental illness of others with rage, retaliation and more violence. Instead use the methods for building happy hormones for yourself, family, community, and the human family world.

Use the blank brain below to inform yourself of your positive and negative APPs. List your techniques learned in this book for reprogramming your brain for social brain healing.

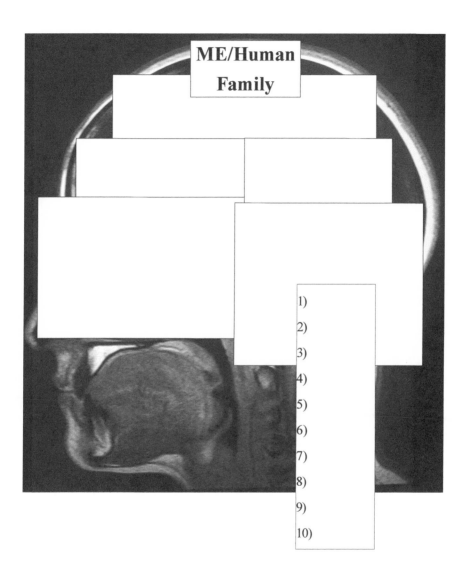

ME/Human Family

1)

2)

3)

4)

5)

6)

7)

8)

9)

10)

REFERENCES

Altman, D., (2011). *One minute mindfulness*. Novato, California: New World Library

Amen, D. G. (1998) *Change your brain change your life: the breakthrough program for conquering anxiety, depression, obsessiveness, anger, and impulsiveness*. New York: Three Rivers Press

Amen, D. G. (2010) *Change your brain change your body*. New York: Three Rivers Press

Anderson, D. E. (1983). Ethnotherapy links ethnic, religious roots to psychological problems. Los Angels Times, United Press International, 4 part I-B.

Arnow, J. (1995). *Teaching peace: How to raise children to live in harmony—without fear, without prejudice, without violence*. New York: Perigee Book

Arden, J. B., & Linford, L. (2009). *Brain-Based therapy with adults*. New Jersey: John Wiley & Sons, Inc.

Arden, J. B., (2010). *Rewire your brain: Think your way to a better life*. New Jersey: John Wiley & Sons, Inc.

Baron, R. A., & Byrne, D., (2003) Social psychology (10th edition). Boston, MA: Allyn and Bacon.

Barry, T. D., Thompson, A., Barry, C. T., Lochman, J. E., Adler, K., & Hill, K. (2007). The importance of narcissism in predicting proactive and reactive aggression in moderately to highly aggressive children. *Aggressive Behavior, 33,* 185 – 197.

Badenoch, B. (2008) *Being a brain-wise therapist: A practical guide to interpersonal neurobiology.* New York: W.W. Norton & Company

Baumeister, R. F., Bushman B. J., & Campbell, W. K. (2000). Self-Esteem, narcissism, and aggression: Does violence result from low self-esteem or from threatened egotism? *Current Direction in Psychological Science, 9,* 26–29.

Baumeister, R. F., Heatherton, T. F., & Tice, D. M. (1993). When ego threats lead to self-regulation failure: Negative consequences of high self-esteem. *Journal of Personality and Social Psychology, 64,* 141–156.

Baumeister, R. F., Smart, L., & Boden, J. M. (1996). Relation of threatened egotism to violence and aggression: The dark side of high self-esteem. *Psychological Review, 103,* 5–33.

Beattie, M. (1987) *Codependent no more: How to stop controlling others and start caring for yourself.* New York: Harper/Hazelden.

ben-Jachannan, Y. A. A., (1987) *The African called Rameses (the great) II and the African Origin of Western Civilization. Black Classic Press: Maryland.*

Berntsen, D., Rubin D., (2002) Emotionally Charged Autobiographical Memories Across the Life Span: The Recall of Happy, Sad, Traumatic, and Involuntary Memories. Psychology and Aging Vol. 17 (4) December, 2002, pp. 636-652.

Boeree, G.C., Personality Theory: A biosocial approach. http:// webspace.ship.edu/cgboer/pt.html

Bowlby, J. (1973). *Attachment and loss: Vol. 2. Separation, anxiety, and anger.* New York: Basic Books

Bushman, B. J., & Baumeister, R. F. (1998). Threatened egotism, narcissism, self-esteem, and direct and displaced aggression: Does self-love or self-hate lead to violence? *Journal of Personality and Social Psychology, 75,* 219-229.

Butterfield, F. (1995) *All God's children: The Bosket family and the American tradition of violence.* New York: Alfred A. Knopf.

Clarke, J. H. (1993) *African people in world history.* Baltimore, MD: Black Classis Press

Cohen J. A. (1981). Theories of narcissism and trauma. *American Journal of Psychotherapy, XXXV,* 93-100.

Crick, N. R., & Dodge, K. A. (1996). Social information-processing mechanisims in reactive and proactive aggression. *Child Development, 67,* 993–1002.

Diop, C. A. (1974). *The African origin of civilization: myth or reality.* Chicago, Illinois: Lawrence Hill Books.

Emmons, R. A. (1984). Factor analysis and construct validity of the narcissistic personality inventory. *Journal of Personality Assessment, 48,* 291–300.

Emmons, R. A. (1987). Narcissism: theory and measurement. *Journal of Personality and Social Psychology, 52,* 11–17.

Farmer, S. D. (2014) Healing ancestral karma: free yourself from unhealthy family patterns. San Antonio, TX: Hierophant Publishing.

Fonagy, P., Gergely, G., Jurist, E. L., & Target, M. (2002). *Affect regulation, mentalizations, and the development of the self.* New York: Other Press.

Fossati, A., Borroni, S., Eisenberg, N., & Maffei, C. (2010). Relations of proactive and reactive dimensions of aggression to overt and covert narcissism in nonclinical adolescents. *Aggressive Behavior, 36,* 21-27. doi: 10.1002/ab.20332

Grier, W. H., & Cobbs, P. M., (2000) *Black rage.* Eugene, OR: Wipf and Stock Publishers.

Garvey, Marcus (2004) *Selected writings of speeches of Marcus Garvey,* edited by Bob Blaisdell. Mineola, New York: Dover Publications, Inc.

Hanson, R. (2011). *Just one thing: developing a Buddha brain one simple practice at a time.* CA: New Harbinger Publications, Inc.

Harman P., Husband C., (1974) *Racism and the Mass Media,* pg. 21.

Hendrix, H. (1988). *Getting the love you want: A guide for couples.* New York: Harper & Row Publishers

Hooks, B. (1995) *Killing rage: Ending racism,* New York: Henry Holt and Company

Howell, E. F., (2003). Narcissism, a relational aspect of dissociation. *Journal of Trauma & Dissociation, 4,* 51-71.

Huther, G. (2004). *The compassionate brain: How empathy creates intelligence.* Boston MA: Trumpeter Books.

Jackson, J. G. (1970). *Introduction to African civilizations.* Secaucus, New Jersey: The Citadel Press.

Jennings, P. (2010). *Mixing Minds.* Boston. Wisdom Publications

James, G. G. M. (1954). *Stolen legacy: the Egyptian origins of western philosophy.* A Traffic Output Publication.

Karen, R. (1994). *Becoming attached.* New York, NY: Oxford University Press

Kagan J. (2010). *The temperamental thread: How genes, culture, time, and luck make us who we are.* New York, NY: The Dana Foundation

Katz, L. C. & Rubin, M. (1999). *Keep your brain alive.* New York: Workman Publishing Company, Inc.

Kernberg, O. F. (2007). The almost untreatable narcissistic patient. *Journal of American Psychoanalytic Association, 55,* 503-539.

Kernis, M. H., & Sun, C. R. (1994). Narcissism and reactions to interpersonal feedback. *Journal of Research in Personality, 28,* 4-13.

Kiyosaki, R.T. & Trump D. (2011). *Midas Touch.* Scottsdale, AZ: Plata Publishing.

Kohut, H. (1972). Thoughts on narcissism and narcissistic rage. *Psychoanalytic Study of the Child, 27,* 360-400.

LaBarre, W., (1954). *The human animal.* Chicago. IL. University of Chicago Press

Lasch, C. L. (1979). *The culture of narcissism.* New York: Norton,

Lester, J. (1968). *To be a slave.* New York: Scholastic Inc.

McHoskey, J. (1995). Narcissism and machiavellianism. *Psychological Reports, 77,* 755-759.

Meltzer, M. (1964). *In their own words: A history of American negro 1619-1865.* New York: Thomas Y. Crowell Company.

Miller, A. (1979). Depression and grandiosity as related forms of narcissistic disturbances. *Int. Rev. Psycho-Anal, 6,* 61.

Miller, A, (2002). *For their own good: Hidden Cruelty in Child-rearing and the Roots of Violence.* Toronto: Collins Publishers.

Monte, C. F. (1980) *Beneath the mask: An introduction to theories of personality (2nd edition).* New York: Holt, Rinehart & Winston.

Morf, C. C., & Rhodewalt, F. (2001). Unraveling the paradoxes of narcissism: A dynamic self-regulatory processing model. *Psychological Inquiry, 12,* 177-196.

Papps, B. P., & O'Carroll, R. E. (1998). Extremes of self-esteem and narcissism and the experience and expression of anger and aggression. *AggressiveBehavior, 24,* 421-438.

Perry, B. D., (1997). Incubated in Terror: Neurodevelopmental Factors in the 'Cycle of Violence' In: *Children, Youth and Violence: The Search for Solutions.* In (J. Osofsky, Ed.). Guilford Press, New York, pp 124-148.

Perry, B. D., (1999). *Memories of fear: How the brain stores and retrieves physiologic states, feelings behaviors, and thoughts from the traumatic events.* Retrieved on 3/2/2007 from The Child Trauma Academy www.trauma-pages.com/perry.

Perry, B. D., (2001). Violence and childhood: How persisting fear can alter the developing child's brain. In Schetky D & Benedek, I. (Eds.) *Textbook of child and adolescent forensic psychiatry.* Washington, D. C.: American Psychiatric Press, Inc. Pp.221-238.

Perry, B. D., Pollard, R. A., Blakley, T. L., Baker, W. L., & Vigilante, D., (1996) Childhood trauma, the neurobiology of adaptation and use-dependent development of the brain: How states becomes traits. *Infant Mental Health Journal.* Retrieved on 1/17/2008, from www.trauma-pages.com/perry

Schore, A. N. (2001). The effects of early relational trauma on right brain development, affect regulation and infant mental health. *Infant Mental Health Journal, 22,* 201-269.

Shelby, S. (1990). The content of our character: A new vision of race in America. New York: St. Martin's Press

Sherwood, V. R. (1990). The first stage of treatment with the conduct disordered adolescent: Overcoming narcissistic resistance. *Psychotherapy: Therapy, Research, Practice, Training, 27,* 380-387.

Shoels, I. (1999). *Isaiah Eamon Shoels.* Retrieved from http://acolumbinesite.com/victim/isaiah.html

Simon, R. I. (2002). Distinguishing trauma-associated narcissistic symptoms from posttraumatic stress disorder: A diagnostic challenge. *Harvard Review of Psychiatry, 10,* 28-36. doi: 10.1093/hrp/10.1.28

Steele, S. (1990). *The content of our character.* St. Martin's Press, New York

Sternberg, B. (2013). *Music and the brain.* Institute for Natural Resources. Concord, NY.

Strengel, R. (2010) *Mandela's way: fifteen lessons on life, love, and courage.* New York: Crown Publishers.

Sullivan B. F., & Geaslin, D. L., (2001). The role of narcissism, self-esteem, and irrational beliefs in predicting aggression. *Journal of Social Behavior and Personality, 16,* 53-68.

Talbott, S. (2002) *The cortisol connection: why stress makes you fat and ruins your health-and what you can do about it.* CA: Hunter House.

Twenge, J. M., & Campbell, W. K. (2003). "Isn't it fun to get the respect that we're going to deserve?" Narcissism, social rejection and aggression. *Personality and Social Psychology Bulletin, 29,* 261-272. doi: 10.1177/0146167202239051

Watson, P.J., Hickman, S.E., Morris, R.J., Milliron, J.T., & Whiting, L. (1995). Narcissism, self-esteem and parental nurturance. *The Journal of Psychology, 129*(1), 61-73.

Whaley, A.L., (2001) Cultural mistrust: An important psychological construct for the diagnosis and treatment of African Americans,

Professional Psychology: Research and Practice, Vol 32 (6). December 2001, p. 555-562, American Psychological Association.

Whaley, A. L. (1998). Cross-cultural perspective on paranoia: A focus on the Black American experience. *Psychiatric Quarterly*, *69*, 325–343.

Williams, C., (1987). *The destruction of black civilization: great issues of a race from 4500 B.C to 2000 A.D.* Chicago, IL: Third World Press.

Wink, P. (1991). Two faces of narcissism. *Journal of Personality and Social Psychology*, *61*, 590–597

Zamostny, K.P, Slyter, S.L. & Rios P. (1993). Narcissistic injury and its relationship to early trauma, early resources, and adjustment to college. *Journal of Counseling Psychology, 40,* 501-510.